RACOVIA

AN EARLY LIBERAL RELIGIOUS COMMUNITY

Phillip Hewett

RACOVIA

AN EARLY LIBERAL RELIGIOUS COMMUNITY

Phillip Hewett

Blackstone Editions, Providence, Rhode Island

Published 2004
Printed in the United States of America

Contents

Preface

There are times and places when the flow of events unleashes the perennial questions that always lurk just below the level of human consciousness. Such thinking may be triggered by a natural catastrophe like the great Lisbon earthquake of 1755, or by horrendous human actions like the Nazi Holocaust during the Second World War. It may, again, be an outcome of the less dramatic but more far-reaching collapse of a whole system of thought through which successive generations have been accustomed to interpret the world and our place in it. In striking words Alfred North Whitehead once described how during his own lifetime, spanning the latter part of the nineteenth century and the first half of the twentieth, all the certainties that had been built up over the course of two and a half centuries upon the foundations laid by Descartes and Newton had come crashing down. "Nothing," he said, "absolutely nothing was left that had not been challenged, if not shaken. This I consider to have been one of the supreme facts of my experience. [It] has affected everything else in the universe for me."

The decades that have passed since Whitehead described this shattering experience have brought no new consensus about the nature of things to replace the one that had been irremediably undermined. Questions rather than answers hover around those who make a sincere attempt to do more than skim the surface of life. Here we are, members of one among the myriad species of living beings on the face of a planet floating in an unimaginably limitless universe. How do we interpret whatever we might suppose to be the scheme of things and our place within it? How do we best relate to one another, and to the world of which we are inextricably a part? With no assured answers, we find ourselves in the situation described by Martin Buber, another philosopher contemporary with Whitehead, when he contrasted epochs of habitation with epochs of homelessness. In the former, human beings live in the universe as in a house, a home. In the latter (and this is our condition today) we are living in the world as in an open field, and at times do not even have four pegs with which to set up a tent.

Under these circumstances, we stand to gain much by listening to those who experienced epochs of homelessness in the past. During the sixteenth century, a medieval consensus that was even more imposing and secure than the Victorian one of Whitehead's early years was collapsing. As in the more recent period, people who were sensitive to this were casting around for a viable alternative, while a majority of the population tried to carry on as though nothing significant was happening. In their everyday lives, the old presuppositions still seemed to work, for the most part.

In that sixteenth-century context, a little band of nonconformists who had become well aware that the old presuppositions were not in fact working for them embarked upon a bold experiment. On a secluded estate in rural Poland they set out to build for themselves a town that was at first intended to be a New Jerusalem – a Utopian community insulated from what was happening in the world at large. When this failed, they attempted more successfully to turn it into a New Rome – a center from which their thinking and practice could exercise an influence upon the life of society at large.

Raków was and is off the beaten track. Yet there was a time when its name became famous all over Europe, mostly on account of the radical thinking embodied in the Racovian Catechism of 1605. The town flourished for less than one human lifespan; yet the ripples arising from this little community have spread in ever-widening circles during the ensuing centuries, and under closer scrutiny their effects can still be seen today.

Chapter 1

A World in Transition

The sixteenth century in Europe was a strange and troubled period of history, in some ways very like our own, in others unutterably remote. The Middle Ages were only gradually giving place to the modern era. It was a time of disruption and transition succeeding a long and settled period of assurance and certitude. We are dealing here with a period before the work of Descartes and Newton and Locke had begun, even before Galileo. The world was still limited in scope. The century opened only eight years after Columbus's first voyage, only two years after Vasco da Gama sailed round the Cape to India. Nearly a quarter of that century had elapsed before the globe was circumnavigated for the first time. Not until 1543, three years before the death of Luther, was the traditional view of the universe first seriously challenged with the publication of Copernicus's *De Revolutionibus*. And less than a century had passed at that time since the invention of printing had smoothed the path for the spread of new ideas.

For the greater part of the century, in spite of the furious conflicts between Catholic and Protestant, in spite of the very real possibility that the Turks would triumphantly carry Islam to all parts of Europe, for most people the closed medieval system still provided the framework within which their thinking was done. The earth was the center of the universe, specially created by God as a home for a human race which had been given dominion over everything upon its surface. Human beings, though fallen and sinful, still occupied a unique place in the scheme of things, intermediate between the exclusively corporeal being of animals and the purely spiritual being of angels, and partaking to some extent of the nature of each. God was revealed both through the evidences of Nature and the pages of Scripture. Everything formed part of one interlocking order, with an exact analogy explaining in turn the nature and structure of each human being, of human society, of the natural world and of the entire universe. As the sixteenth-century writer Annibale Romei put it, "The body of man is no other but a little model of the sensible world, and his soul an image of the world intelligible."

Such a synthesis was not easily overthrown, even in face of discoveries that threw its validity into question. Except to a few venturesome and original thinkers, it had the advantages of credibility and simplicity. It was venerable and sanctified by the authority of church and state. It explained most of the experiences that came the way of most people. Most important of all, it gave those who embraced it a sense of being at home in the universe. It may not at times have been a very comfortable home, but it was better than the sense of aloneness in a vast and incomprehensible universe that so terrified Pascal a century later.

But the walls of this imposing home were already beginning to be undermined. Nicholas Copernicus, working quietly away in Poland, has become a symbolic figure in this connection, as expressed in the term "Copernican revolution." But the full significance of what he was proposing escaped the notice of the Catholic authorities even in those turbulent days, and many years passed before his book was placed on the Index of prohibited reading. The Protestant leaders scented the danger more immediately. Luther denounced Copernicus in typically scathing language: "People give ear to an upstart astrologer who strove to show that the earth revolves, not the heaven or the firmament, the sun and the moon ... This fool wishes to reverse the entire science of astronomy, but sacred scripture tells us that Joshua commanded the sun to stand still and not the earth." Calvin's response was similar, asking, "Who will venture to place the authority of Copernicus above that of the Holy Spirit?"

Copernicus, however, was only one of the subverters of the old system. In the same year as his book was published, Vesalius published his researches into human anatomy, discrediting Galen and the long-revered authorities. Machiavelli's cynical but realistic account of the ways in which human societies are actually governed undermined the established view that they were divinely ordained according to a pattern laid up in the heavens. Montaigne gave utterance to an all-embracing skepticism that left none of the traditional structures intact. These and other challengers of the traditional view of things were eagerly read and discussed all across Europe. Theological dogmas could obviously not be exempted from this process of free inquiry, particularly since they interlocked so neatly with many of the presuppositions of the obsolescent sciences.

But old habits die hard. The Catholic church, when at length it grasped the extent of the threat posed by the new thinking and mustered its resources to fight, was able to gather widespread support because most people, despite their misgivings, were still locked into the presuppositions of the old system. Even the radicals who represented the vanguard of progress could not be expected to leap in one generation from medieval thinking to that of, say, the eighteenth-century Enlightenment. It is scarcely surprising that the earliest radicals, having rejected the authority of the Pope and the church, still accepted the authority of the Bible without question, and hinged their arguments against upholders of the traditionally accepted views upon biblical quotations, often taken out of context.

Critical study of the Bible was then scarcely in its infancy, and it does them an injustice if they are accused of not being aware of what took several generations of painstaking research to unravel. The more recent acquaintance with the existence of the scriptures of other world religions, each with its rival claim to be a revealed authority, puts the Christian scripture in an altogether different perspective from that characteristic of an age when the only other religions widely known were Judaism and Islam. Jews of course accepted much of the same Bible, while Muslims accorded it a respected if not central position in their own faith.

Though the more radical thinkers had taken relatively few steps away from the traditional religious thinking, there were few safe havens for them during this period. The exception was Poland. During what has generally been called its "Golden Age" in the sixteenth century, Poland was renowned throughout Europe as "the heretics' asylum" *(asilum haereticorum).* This word "heretic" was the one thrown by the Catholic church at all dissenters, but the major Protestant bodies in turn were willing to use it against more radical dissenters. As a matter of fact the welcome mat in Poland was a broad one, for Catholics fleeing persecution in the British Isles and elsewhere also found sanctuary there.

This remarkable degree of hospitality to varying religious opinions and practices was approached only in the neighboring states of Moravia and Transylvania, before they succumbed to the Habsburgs' promotion of the Counter-Reformation. Elsewhere in Europe during this period those whose line of thinking did not concur with that of the established authorities were likely to find themselves in a dungeon, torture chamber or place of execution. The proto-Unitarian Michael Servetus was burned at the stake in Protestant Geneva in 1553. Another distinguished fellow-pioneer, Jacob Palaeologus, suffered the same fate in Rome in 1585. One did not necessarily have to take as radical a stance as this to be put to death. The whole epoch was marked by wars of religion, with Catholics killing Protestants and Protestants killing Catholics. In France alone, bloody encounters culminated in the St Bartholomew's Eve massacre in 1572, when at least 20,000 Protestants were butchered in cold blood by Catholics.

By contrast, Poland during this period recorded no more than one or two deaths attributable to religious discord, and civil disturbances were unusual. Toleration arose out of a number of circumstances that favored its growth. The Polish-Lithuanian Commonwealth, to give it its proper title, was the largest and most diversified country in Europe. It came into being as a result of a dynastic marriage in 1385 which brought the two countries together under one monarch. This was not a particularly unusual situation – Poland and Hungary, for instance, had a single monarch from 1440 to 1444; Bohemia and Hungary from

1490 to 1526. But the Polish-Lithuanian combination continued, despite the fact that the monarchy was elective and not automatically hereditary, and in 1569 it was consummated into a full federation between the two countries. The population within this vast area, which included the whole of what are now Belarus and Ukraine, was from the outset divided between the Roman Catholic and the Eastern Orthodox churches. It also included a considerable Muslim element, as well as what rapidly became the largest Jewish community in Europe. The Reformation period added Lutherans, Calvinists, Hussites, Mennonites and other Anabaptists, and in due course the emerging movement which became Unitarian. Peace between these multifarious groups was the only practical alternative to disastrous civil strife, and this was readily perceived by those in a position to influence the course of events.

Economic motivations were also at work. Heretics who sought asylum in Poland brought with them skills that enriched the life of the country. The marshes in the Vistula delta were drained by Dutch Mennonites; Anabaptists from Germany brought a faience pottery industry; Italian professionals contributed to medicine, education and the arts.

Even without the immigrants, religious diversity was growing in Poland. Well-to-do families sent their sons to universities in Italy and other Western countries, and they often returned with an outlook reflecting Renaissance humanism or Reformation Protestantism. They did not in consequence run afoul of the established authorities, because they and their families were in fact the established authorities. Poland was, to be sure, a monarchy, and its kings during this period were fully prepared to live with religious diversity. King Sigismund I, who reigned from 1506 to 1548, memorably declared: "Please permit me to be king of both the sheep and the goats!" while his son and successor, Sigismund Augustus, told the assembled parliament, "I shall not place burdens on anyone's conscience; in truth, that is not my intention, for it is not my task to create religion."

In actual fact, he had quite limited power to decide otherwise. Toleration was not dependent, as in some other countries, upon royal proclamations. Poland's monarchs were democratically elected. Such a democracy rested upon a franchise limited to members of the *szlachta,* the nobility, but these comprised up to ten percent of the entire population, a figure that was not even approached in most parts of the Continent. Furthermore, there were no subdivisions of aristocratic rank such as existed elsewhere, with dukes and counts and marquises and barons. The only distinction between them was one of wealth and influence. At one end of the scale, some members of the *szlachta* owned very little land and had to work it themselves; at the other end of the scale were the magnates, the greatest of whom owned vast territories with hundreds of villages and thousands of serfs. In the two houses of the Parliament, the Chamber of Deputies consisted of members elected by the *szlachta* at local assemblies, where members of magnate families were often able to exert enough influence to secure their own election. The Senate was composed on the one hand of senior members of the Catholic hierarchy (whose own status had been subject to royal approval), and on the other hand of officials appointed by the king in consultation with the power elite: palatines and castellans who were supposedly responsible for regional administration. In practice, these were almost always the wealthiest magnates, whom it would have been politically imprudent for the king to pass over in making appointments. Legislation was endorsed in joint sessions of the Senate and Chamber of Deputies, subsequently approved by the king.

The proportion of the population entitled to vote was roughly the same as in ancient Athens, which was often cited as a precedent, for Athenian democracy rested in fact upon a large substratum of disenfranchised slaves, as did the democracy of the early period in the United States. Polish royal elections could draw a turnout as high as 40,000, and were sometimes sharply contested, even occasionally to the point of armed conflict.

The state was highly decentralized. This was true even of the army; besides the armed forces under the direct control of the king there were substantial forces controlled by the greater magnates. While all sections of the social structure worked together in face of a clear external threat, the military could not normally be used as a tool for internal repression and the establishment of an autocratic state.

Toleration may often have been a policy of expediency, but it spared Poland the horrors of the wars of religion that devastated much of Europe in the sixteenth century. Moreover, there were within all parties some for whom it was more of a principle than an expedient. These, whether Catholics or Protestants, had been deeply influenced by Renaissance humanism. The most distinguished figure of the times, Andrew Frycz Modrzewski, was much influenced by Erasmus of Rotterdam, whose library he brought to its purchaser John Łaski in Poland after Erasmus's death. He was an influential author as well as serving for a while as the king's secretary, and remained a Catholic throughout his life, though his thinking brought him close to the early Unitarians. He argued forcefully for religious toleration, as did many other individuals. But perhaps the most notable declaration on this subject was the one in which the whole parliament *(Sejm)* joined in 1573, constituting itself the Confederation of Warsaw: "Whereas there is a great dissidence in the affairs of the Christian religion in our country, and to prevent any sedition for this reason among the people such as we clearly perceive in other realms, we swear to each other, on behalf of ourselves and our descendants, in perpetuity ... that we who differ in matters of religion will keep the peace among ourselves, and neither shed blood on account of differences of faith, or kinds of church, nor punish one another by confiscation of goods, deprivation of honor, imprisonment or exile."

History is of course replete with examples of noble declarations that are not implemented in practice. But this remained the official policy of the Polish state for many years. The degree of security that heretics actually enjoyed varied from one place to another. On the estates of sympathetic members of the *szlachta* such security was almost complete. It was much less so in the cities or on the estates owned by the Catholic church, and as the sixteenth century gave place to the seventeenth, it progressively declined everywhere. But the sixteenth century was indeed a Golden Age.

This was particularly true for the most radical of all the heretics, who created the tradition within which the Racovian experiment belonged. That tradition bore a variety of names, many of them labels attached by opponents in an attempt to discredit it. Within the Christian context in which this new departure took place, its adherents were tarred with the names of ancient Christian heresies that had been denounced for centuries. The resemblance to those heresies, while not totally imaginary, was often as superficial as that which caused the early European settlers in North America to call a bird a robin simply because, like the European bird of that name, it had a red breast.

Thus it came about that these early pioneers were called Photinians, Samosatenists, Sabellians and (most commonly) Arians, after the fourth-century heretic Arius, to whose views theirs had at least some points of similarity. That label has persisted in Poland right down to the present day. In the wider European context they were often called Socinians, after Faustus Socinus, who was their chief spokesperson during the latter part of his life, though he was never formally a member. They were also frequently referred to as Anabaptists, as a consequence of their having adopted adult baptism as the initiation rite into their community. But this was never universally practiced among them, and their views were very different from those of the majority streams of Anabaptism such as the Mennonites.

None of these names was accepted by the people so designated. The name they themselves used was "Polish Brethren," to which during the latter part of their history they added "Unitarian" – a term that had originated in nearby Transylvania and has been carried by the movement they pioneered down to the present day in many parts of the world. As a matter of convenience this is the terminology that will be used here, describing as it does not only their theology but also the principles they shared with Unitarians of subsequent centuries, notably those of freedom, reason and tolerance in matters of religion. But one of the paradoxes of Unitarian history is that its adherents, unlike those of most traditions, often show relatively little interest in those who went before them in their own movement, except to mention with pride those who attained some fame in the world at large.

Chapter 2

Humanists and Communists

Two types of response to the breakdown of the old order in the sixteenth century went into the making of the Unitarian movement. They were presented by Earl Morse Wilbur in his *History of Unitarianism,* elaborating upon a thesis first advanced by the Italian scholar Francesco Ruffini.

First, there were those whose chief concern was to re-create the sense of community that had been shattered. They had little concern for the speculations of theology, still less of philosophy, but were in search of a way of life that amid all the rapidly-evolving conditions of the age would express what they understood to be the will of God. These were the left wing of the Protestant Reformation, the Anabaptists, not by any means a homogeneous group, but all sharing this very practical orientation, this burning sense of a need to do something immediately to make it possible to live as true Christians even within a world of disruption – or, as most of them believed, dissolution.

The other response was that of persons who had wholeheartedly embraced the spirit of the Renaissance, naturally enough in the first generation nearly all of them Italians. Their view of the new era was not shaped by any injury inflicted by it upon them; in fact, they were its beneficiaries. It had liberated them and opened all kinds of doors that had hitherto been closed. Injuries they would in due course receive, but those of which they were most conscious in the first period were the ones aimed at them by the Roman Catholic church and its agents wherever and whenever their thinking passed beyond the accepted boundaries. Wilbur identified them as "the Humanists south of the Alps." They were, he wrote, "cultivated individuals of high social position and superior education ... they were relatively as few in number as they were important in influence. In temperament they were rationalists and their primary interest in religion was intellectual. The Christian religion was to them a system of philosophy, and the Church a school of definite and reasonable opinions."

Such were the two streams that appeared in the middle years of the century. "It will at once be imagined," Wilbur continued, "that if these two groups could in the course of time and by natural processes be somehow fused, a very interesting religious movement might result, and one stronger than either of its component parts. Such a fusion was in fact destined to take place in Poland."

Subsequent events in Poland as well as in the Unitarian bodies that later emerged elsewhere lend support to this thesis. The bipolar nature of the movement appears in various ways, of which the tension between the claims of individuality and those of community is the most significant in the context being considered here. A concern for the integrity of one's own individuality had begun to flower as one aspect of the Renaissance, and resulted in demands for what were seen as the human rights of each person. But none of us is an isolated individual – "an island entire of itself," as John Donne memorably put it a century later. The idea that human beings were in fact islands of this kind in the most primitive stage of their evolution, and later brought an ordered society into being by a "social contract," gained wide support in the early modern period, but has resulted in a degree of alienation for the individual that has had many disastrous consequences. Yet the alternative view which submerges individuality in a collectivity like that of ants and bees has been strenuously and with good reason resisted. Unitarians have wrestled with this dilemma ever since the sixteenth century.

Other polarities that could be cited are those between the rational approach that analyses and divides and the mystical approach that synthesizes and unites; between the intellectual emphasis that concerns itself with a pursuit of elusive truths and the practical approach that is concerned with promoting social change; between encouragement of freedom of thought and room to grow, and the need to express firm convictions as a basis for meaningful living.

Ruffini's identification of the two streams which merged deserves a little closer attention. The Italian humanists who made their way to Poland were typical of their class – typical in all respects except that they took their view of religion so seriously that they were prepared to face exile and even death rather than betray it. Like all educated Italians of their time, they were exposed to the rediscovered art and letters of the classical world, they were very pronounced individualists, experimenters and freethinkers, and they had an optimistic view of the possibilities of human nature. Where they differed from most of their contemporaries was in feeling compelled to take religion seriously, a trait they shared with the otherwise dissimilar Protestant reformers to the north.

Individualism combined with this powerful interest in religion drove them inevitably into opposition to the established forms of religion, which in Italy meant the Roman Catholic Church. At first they tried to avoid and circumvent the established church as far as possible, rather than attempting to destroy and replace it, like the German reformers. They were, said Delio Cantimori, "rebels against every kind of ecclesiastical communion," seeing religion as a matter between each individual and God, not to be compromised by the demands of any institution. After the re-establishment of the Italian Inquisition in 1542 their position became more and more perilous and untenable. The many Polish students at Italian universities absorbed the same attitudes, and gave leadership to the radical school of thinking in their own country that was well under way even before the arrival of refugees from Italy.

The second component in the fusion in Poland, that of the Anabaptists, was part of a religious faction that was no more homogeneous as a whole than were the humanists. For centuries this form of religion had to suffer abuse heaped upon it by opponents, who in most cases were only too eager to place all its adherents in the same category as the fanatical Anabaptists who caused such havoc when they seized control of the city of Münster in 1534.

Some characteristics were indeed shared by the movement as a whole. All opposed the traditional Christian practice of infant baptism – hence the very name they were given. All (except the Münster extremists) favored the complete separation of church and state and opposed the use of armed violence. All endorsed social justice, a sharing of the material goods given by God, though there was no unanimity as to the way in which this was to be done. Nor was there unanimity regarding the payment of taxes levied for what they would consider immoral purposes, notably the waging of war. All these characteristics illustrate the serious manner in which the practical demands of religious living were viewed.

After very severe persecutions during the first thirty years of their existence as a separate stream in the religious life of Europe, the Anabaptists divided into two main groups, which have persisted to the present day: Mennonites and Hutterites. Both these groups appear remote in most respects from the later Unitarian movement, and few persons unacquainted with the earlier history would have supposed that at one time there was a very close dialogue, even, in the eyes of some people, looking towards an organic union. Yet such was the case. Dialogue with the Mennonites was mostly confined to the seventeenth century and had little impact upon Unitarian evolution, but the dialogue with the Hutterites was an important element in the earliest period of Unitarian organization. These sixteenth-century communists had a magnetic attraction for many of its leading figures, who could fairly be described as being themselves Anabaptists.

It was a general accusation against Anabaptists that they advocated and practiced a complete community of goods – full communism – but in fact it was only the Hutterites who followed such a practice. Most Anabaptists retained private property, looking upon it as a sacred trust held from God not only for the use of the actual possessor, but for the benefit of all. Voluntary assistance to others in need, rather than community of goods, expressed their religious ideal. Menno Simons, after whom the Mennonites took their name, said that Anabaptists "entertain those in distress. They take the stranger into their home. They comfort the afflicted; assist the needy; clothe the naked; feed the hungry; do not turn their face from the poor." This was not based upon any alleged right of the recipient to receive such help; the entire stress lay upon the need to give as an expression of religious commitment.

The Hutterites, however, constituted the radical wing of Anabaptism, just as the Anabaptists were the radical wing of the Reformation. They were refugees from Germany and Switzerland, and more especially from the Austrian Tirol, who had fled to Moravia, the eastern province of the kingdom of Bohemia. Though this was by that time under Habsburg rule, it was far enough from the center of power for the landed aristocracy to preserve a fair degree of their traditional autonomy. They welcomed the Anabaptists as hard and efficient workers who would bring back life and wealth to an area that had been depopulated by war, famine and disease. There was therefore a precarious convergence of interests. The landowners saw a source of wealth and power for themselves from the contributions to the economy the new colonists would make; the Anabaptists were grateful to find a place of refuge from the unspeakable tortures being visited upon them further west.

They organized themselves into communes where all material goods would be held in common. Though it soon became evident that this form of economic organization was a very efficient one, their original motivation was not at all economic. They simply felt impelled by the demands of their religion to live in this way. From various passages in the Bible they deduced that this was in accordance with the will of God, the most noteworthy text in this connection being the passage in the *Acts of the Apostles* that said of the earliest Christians: "all that believed were together, and had all things common."

The initial steps to establish community of goods took place as early as 1528. At first, there were some problems; it was alleged that the preachers were taking unfair advantage of the community of goods, living at a much higher standard than the rest of the community. There was probably some substance to this complaint, for it was echoed at a later date by the Unitarians from Poland who investigated the communes at first hand, but Jacob Huter, leader of the movement, reorganized the communes in a very tightly-knit manner. There were rigid inspections to ensure that everything became the property of the community as a whole. Excommunication was the penalty for anyone caught cheating, and Huter did not hesitate to enforce this upon one of the leading figures. Not only were meals eaten in common and consumer goods allocated to individuals for their personal use while remaining the property of the commune as a whole, but work was also undertaken communally. The various tasks were assigned by the whole community, and the individual members were expected to accept whatever was allocated to them without question. Each family had its own living quarters, which in effect meant sleeping quarters, and these were changed and allocated according to the size of the family. With practically no change, this is precisely the form of social organization to be found in the Hutterite communities on the Canadian prairies to this day.

In their heyday, the Hutterite communes in Moravia numbered as many as sixty-five at any given time, with many thousands of members. Few of them had any high standard of education, but on the other hand they were not, as some opponents have alleged, the dregs of society for whom the standard of living they found in the commune could not fail to be an improvement over what they had before. They were mostly skilled artisans, people who could have made their way independently in the world had it not been for their religious convictions. They may have had other motivations of which they were not consciously aware. There was the psychological need for fellowship among the faithful in face of a hostile, menacing and ever-changing world, particularly since they constituted isolated German-speaking colonies in a Czech-speaking country. Or again, considering the condition of destitution to which they had been reduced before they arrived and to which they were more than once reduced again by later persecutions, this may have been the most effective way of staying alive. But they were sure of what their conscious motivation was, and articulated it very clearly. In short, they believed that their way of life was prescribed for them directly by God and that it was an indispensable part of the road to salvation.

The Hutterites never established themselves in Poland. But being so close at hand and on the direct route to and from Italy, they soon became known to the radical spirits in the Polish Reformation, and some at least of their ideas were appropriated by the rising proto-Unitarian movement.

The humanists and the Hutterian communists, therefore, were each in their own way trying to make some sense out of the new and bewildering world in which they found themselves. Both comprised people who took their religion very seriously, though in the one case religion was an attempt to make sense of life at an intellectual level, while in the other it was an attempt to make sense of life at a practical level. Too much stress should not be laid upon this disjunction, though it was a real one. Ruffini's polarity between the Humanists and the Anabaptists does provide a working basis for contrasting the intellectual, analytic approach with the emotional, synthetic one. Though there were many who exemplified both approaches, there were also many whose personal orientation lay almost exclusively in one direction or the other. On the one hand, there were skeptical intellectual dilettantes who often ended up in a refusal to take anything seriously; on the other hand, there were anti-intellectual but morally-concerned persons who accepted the ethical demands of everyday living without ever lifting their heads to confront the vastness of the universe and ask what it was all about.

Those who created the Unitarian tradition felt the pull of both these polarities and attempted to find an effective response to what they felt. In theology, they had already moved a lot further from inherited traditions than their contemporaries, guided by an application of reason to those traditions and to life as a whole, but they were still influenced more than they knew by presuppositions inherited from the Middle Ages that were more difficult to shake off than specific dogmas may have been. In their social concerns, they were not dependent completely upon the Anabaptists for their inspiration. There were other influences that were equally significant. Whereas the Anabaptists from choice or necessity made their social experiments within their own closed communities, these others tended to direct their attention to the reformation of society as a whole.

The vision of such reformers is vividly portrayed in the work of Sir Thomas More in England, whose famous book *Utopia* was published in 1516, circulated in several European languages, and gave its name to a whole stream of thought. The poles between which his thinking moved – practical statecraft and imaginative construction of an ideal community – are typical of the humanist orientation. The Italian humanists were greatly influenced by Plato's *Republic* and by Leonardo da Vinci's designs for an ideal city, which did not seem far beyond the range of possibility in the euphoria that gripped the Italian city-states. The chief expositor of this position in Poland was Andrew Frycz Modrzewski, whose *De Republica Emendanda* was published in Cracow in 1551 and was quickly reprinted both in its original Latin and in various translations in different parts of Europe. Frycz Modrzewski was in a sense the Sir Thomas More of Poland, a man for all seasons, though he had the good fortune to live in a country where independent thinking did not cost him his head. His book did not, like More's, portray an imaginary idealized realm, but took the form of specific proposals for political reform as the outcome of a reassessment of the values that should govern all human societies. He called for a system of law that would apply impartially to all citizens without distinction of rank; in the same way the onerous burden of taxation should be taken off the backs of the peasants. The state should sponsor a system of public education, financed by taxation of all properties, including those of the Church. He praised the Polish system of elected and responsible monarchs, with power resting with the parliament. In international affairs, he opposed warfare as a policy, except where it was forced upon a state in self-defense.

Not content with proposing a re-ordering of the affairs of the state, he proceeded to advocate similar reforms for the church. It should be a national body embracing both Catholics and Protestants, though committed to theological orthodoxy. Bishops should be elected and there should be freedom of conscience. Priests should be allowed to marry. Such proposals resulted in his book's being banned by the Vatican, just as the political proposals resulted in his being hounded from office, though he was permitted to live quietly on his own estates.

In many of these ideas, Frycz Modrzewski was following the lead of his mentor Erasmus, particularly in stressing the need to think things through carefully, even when such careful consideration might delay action. The debate between these theorists and the activists who argued that time did not permit of such intellectual niceties illustrated the perpetual tension in Unitarian and other progressive circles between liberals and radicals. Then as now human progress requires both approaches, but often this fact has been obscured in internecine struggle, with the radicals regarding the liberals as accomplices of the reactionaries, and the liberals regarding the radicals as reckless and unthinking fanatics.

Chapter 3

A New Community

Amid all these polarities, the Unitarian movement arose in Poland as the outcome of a process that had been developing for a good many years. The Reformation there had followed the same course as in other parts of the Continent, spreading first in its Lutheran form and then increasingly in its Calvinist form. The Bohemian Brethren, a Hussite group outlawed in its native land, was also represented. These movements made most of their converts among the powerful *szlachta,* as well as in the very small class of bourgeoisie in the cities, which had relatively little influence in the country's power structure. Some of the peasantry followed the lead of the gentry on whose estates they lived, but the mass of the people stayed with the Roman Catholic Church in Poland itself or with the Orthodox Church in the vast eastern territories of the Polish-Lithuanian Commonwealth. Politically, the Protestants were a force to be reckoned with, comprising nearly one-quarter of the entire *szlachta* and almost a majority at times in the parliaments. Most of them by far were Calvinists, and it was among the Calvinists that the ferment began out of which the "Arian" movement emerged.

The first overt step in its formation came on January 22, 1556, when the Reformed churches of Poland (the Calvinists) assembled for their synod in the little town of Secemin. Consternation reigned when a bombshell was dropped by a man named Peter Giezek from Goniądz, referred to in the Latin controversies of the time as Gonesius. He rose in the assembly and attacked the doctrine of the Trinity and the

Athanasian Creed. He proclaimed the undivided unity of God and declared that Christ was an inferior being to the Father, though indeed he was more than a man and had existed before the creation of the world. This point of view was similar to, though not identical with, that of the early Christian heretic Arius, and provided the pretext for the term "Arian" which was attached to the later Polish movement by its opponents and has continued in popular usage. By the time the movement became organized, it was already passing beyond the theological position staked out by Gonesius, so the name was more emotive than descriptive in meaning.

Gonesius combined in one person the Humanist and Anabaptist approaches. He was born in northeastern Poland, on the borders of Lithuania, around 1530, and after graduating from the University of Cracow was sent by the Bishop of Wilno (Vilnius) to pursue his studies in Italy. He spent four years at the University of Padua, where he gained a doctorate and a lectureship in logic. At Padua he was exposed to all the currents of thought circulating among the Italian humanists of the day, and became a close friend of one of the most heretical among them, Matteo Gribaldi, the university's Professor of Law. Through Gribaldi he became acquainted with the writings of Michael Servetus, whose theological radicalism, particularly his rejection of the traditional Christian doctrine of the Trinity, had led to his having been burned at the stake in Calvin's Geneva in 1553. The influence of Servetus is readily apparent in Gonesius's subsequent confessions of faith, so much so that Luther's friend and colleague Melanchthon was moved to comment that he was evidently bent upon trying to bring Servetus back from hell.

Having absorbed so thoroughly the humanist spirit of Padua, and shared the exile which heresy brought upon his friend and mentor in 1555, Gonesius returned to Lithuania by way of Moravia, where he spent some time at the Hutterite commune in Slavkov (Austerlitz). The social teachings of the Hutterites appealed to him as much as did the theological views of Servetus and the Italian heretics. Their most immediately obvious effect upon him was that he abandoned the sword which in those days was part of the standard dress of the nobility, and carried instead a wooden sword, patterned on the plain staff of the Hutterites, as a token of his pacifism.

It was not only pacifism, however, that he imbibed from the Hutterites. Like them, he accepted the alleged communism of the early Christians as the true pattern of a Christian society, in which all social and political activities should be completely subordinated to the requirements of the Gospel. He opposed the institution of private property, accepted the common Anabaptist view that a Christian should not accept public office under the state (which might involve the performance of legally-required actions in violation of the demands of conscience), and opposed the use of force under all circumstances. Naturally, he also rejected infant baptism.

All these issues were to be vigorously debated in Poland during the next few decades, but it was Gonesius who first brought them to the forefront of public attention. He appears to have been an attractive personality, an incarnation of the humanist model, presenting his views through calm and dignified reasoning, by contrast with the virulent name-calling into which theological controversies so often degenerated at that time. The former Catholic bishop Pier Paolo Vergerio, who debated with him, said of him, "He is a learned and subtle man."

He was persuasive enough to bring a number of his hearers at the synod in Secemin to his point of view, but he did not become the active leader of a party. In fact, he was soon outdistanced, theologically at any rate, by those he had stimulated into doing their own pioneering in these realms. He withdrew to his own comparatively remote part of the country, where he settled on the estate of a sympathetic noble and continued to minister to a small congregation until his death, probably in 1571.

The most immediate and obvious result of the thinking he set in motion was a widening split in the Reformed Church. More and more of its outstanding and articulate leaders began to expound similar ideas, and were opposed by the conservatives, backed by the Protestant leaders in Switzerland and Germany. At first these disputes were mostly theological, concerned with the nature of God and of Christ, and with the doctrine of the Trinity, which the radicals dismissed as unscriptural.

Each synod was marked by such debates, accompanied by a flood of writings.

As a result of the spread of heretical ideas in Poland, as well as the tolerance of the government, a number of the Italian humanists who were by now being hounded all over Europe began to arrive. Of these the most outstanding were Laelius Socinus and Giorgio Biandrata, who arrived in 1558; Giorgio Negri, who was there a year earlier and was appointed pastor to an Italian congregation in Pinczów; his father Francesco Negri who followed him in 1563; Gianpaolo Alciati de la Motta, who came late in 1562 and was followed a few months later by his friend Giovanni Gentile; and Bernardino Ochino, one of the most famous heretics of his day, who arrived the following year. To these should be added Nicola Paruta, who, although he only visited Poland briefly, had a continuing part in the story there. These notable reinforcements to liberal humanism in the country's religious life naturally speeded its growth.

The beleaguered conservatives, both Calvinist and Catholic, turned to the civil power for help, and succeeded in achieving one of the few lapses in toleration during this period. The king and parliament were persuaded to issue in 1564 the Edict of Parczów, decreeing that foreign apostates from the Catholic church who had come to Poland and were spreading new teachings should be banished forthwith. Biandrata, who of all those mentioned had stayed longest and probably had the greatest influence, had already left for Transylvania the previous year. The persons most immediately threatened were Alciati, Gentile and Ochino, and they all promptly set out to join Paruta at Slavkov in Moravia, in close proximity to one of the largest Hutterite communes. Alciati, while there, wrote back to Poland an enthusiastic account of the Hutterite way of life, which commended their views on baptism.

Events in Poland moved rapidly towards a complete schism within the Reformed Church. A last-ditch attempt to avert this was made early in 1565, when the parliament met at Piotrków. With the consent of the king, who was anxious not to see the nation weakened by further religious dissensions, a debate was held between the conservative and radical factions to see whether some mutually acceptable compromise could be reached. But all to no avail: the hard-line Calvinists grew more and more insulting as the debates proceeded without convincing their opponents to yield. In the end they called the radicals Satans, blasphemers and traitors to the country, and broke off the debate. The king, trying to make some sense of what had happened, commissioned Frycz Modrzewski as his secretary to make a summary of the arguments – thinking perhaps that if they were written down by someone with such a reasonable mind there might still be a way out. The only result was a very fine book, *Sylvae*, which Frycz Modrzewski sent to Basel to be printed by an old friend of his. A leading Polish Calvinist, Christopher Trecy, who was in Basel at the time, persuaded the printer to lend him the manuscript and carried it off. On his return to Poland, he shamelessly denied all knowledge of what had happened to it. Fortunately Frycz Modrzewski had kept his notes and was able to reconstruct it. It was later printed on the Unitarian press at Raków as a valuable contribution to their cause.

But the break was complete. A new religious body had come into being, carrying with it most of the leadership of the Polish Reformed Church but only a minority of the membership. It was at first called the Minor Reformed Church of Poland, though in the course of its history it was given a wide variety of names: Arians, Antitrinitarians, Socinians and a number of other labels that were little more than terms of abuse. By the end of the century they were generally speaking of themselves as *Bracia Polscy* (Polish Brethren) and during the last period of their existence they began to use the Unitarian name. Their final literary bequest to the world, a massive collection of their printed works, was published under the title *The Library of the Polish Brethren who are called Unitarians.*

Whatever name may be used to speak of it, the new independent body assembled for the first time as a separate entity in the town of Brzeziny on June 10, 1565. "This date," wrote Earl Morse Wilbur, "may therefore be taken as that of the historical beginning of organized Unitarianism." This and other early meetings were concerned largely with theological issues, but soon social and ethical questions began to come to the fore, and proved as controversial within the new church as theology had been in the old one. It was partly as a response to this that the more radical spirits began to think in terms of building their own New Jerusalem, a place in which life could proceed on the lines they believed were demanded by a true allegiance to the spirit of Christianity – the same motivation as had led the Hutterites to establish their communes.

Chapter 4

The Red Crayfish

In a remote area of south-central Poland, between the cities of Kielce and Sandomierz, lay a district of gently rolling hills, with mixed fields and forests and a light sandy soil, not too fertile, but capable of a reasonable return for care and effort. The landowner here was John Sienieński, a Calvinist magnate whose outlook expressed the tolerant tradition of the Polish *szlachta.* His wife, Jadwiga Gnoińska, had in fact already become a member of the Minor Church. The idea of founding a new town appears to have been a joint project, for the name chosen, Raków, was taken from the Gnoiński family's coat of arms. This depicted a red crayfish on a white background, and became the coat of arms of the town. That choice had consequences that were probably not foreseen, for the Polish word *rak,* crayfish, is also the word for cancer, and after the town became a Unitarian center this gave their opponents a field day. Thus the Catholic writer Powodowski, an inveterate enemy of the Polish Brethren, described Raków as a cancerous ulcer spreading its poison far and wide.

It is questionable whether John Sienieński had at the outset any intention of sponsoring what became known in due course as the Unitarian capital of Europe. The building of new towns on virgin soil was not an infrequent occurrence in those days, and was usually undertaken by the landowner as an investment from which he hoped to gain economically. These were known as private cities. The land on which they stood remained the property of the proprietor, who was thereby in a position to dominate decisions as to what should take place there.

Whatever his motives, on March 27, 1567, having obtained a special mandate from the king, John Sieniński issued a charter for the establishment of a new town to be known as Raków. It contained generous provisions as an inducement to potential settlers. In addition to the freedoms enjoyed by the inhabitants of royal cities as distinct from private ones, it promised freedom from all payments, rents and levies for the first twenty years.

It provided also for free pasturage for the inhabitants' cattle on land adjacent to the town, and for enough land attached to each house to provide adequate gardens. Permission was even given to use the neighboring woods and forests "at any time to meet any needs." Local government would be in the hands of a council of six members, two of them appointed by himself, the other four elected by the inhabitants.

But the most unusual and significant provision was as follows: "I therefore proclaim ... that upon none of the aforesaid Racovians who profess a faith in which they differ from others do I wish to impose any rule from myself, nor upon any of their successors or subjects; nor will I permit my administrators to rule over them, but to each of them, until the Lord shall give them his grace and bring them to the unity of the faith in life eternal, do I promise in my name and in the name of my successors to let them remain in their faith, and this I promise."

In spite of such inducements, there was no immediate influx of settlers. The rural population at that time was composed of freeholders farming their own land or serfs tied to their masters' estates; the former had little incentive to move and the latter had no freedom to do so. As for the artisans and professionals in the cities, they too had little incentive to move to a remote place where the demand for their services was a totally unknown quantity. In consequence, little or nothing appears to have happened for a couple of years, and the founding of the town is dated not from 1567, but from 1569.

In that year a great deal happened. The problems just mentioned are drastically reduced when a large number of people move all at once, under the influence of motives other than purely economic ones. The seething discussion with regard to the lifestyle demanded of individuals who took their religion seriously came to a boil. Many wanted to find a community where they could live as authentically as they believed the Hutterites to do. In addition to this internal pressure, they were beginning to feel the external pressure of persecution. The frustrated Calvinists lost no opportunity of trying to punish the radicals for their apostasy, while the Catholic Church, which had for so long been on the defensive as more and more of its leaders joined the Reformation, now began to recover its strength again. Cardinal Hosius, who had had a prominent role at the Council of Trent, began a long and carefully planned campaign to overthrow Protestantism in all its forms, starting with those who would be least likely to be able to rally others to their defense. The Jesuits, who were the standard-bearers of the Counter-Reformation, were introduced into Poland in 1564. Already by the end of that decade, there were places that were becoming uncomfortable, even unsafe, for heretics, in spite of all the safeguards embodied in the law. The result was a large-scale migration of the more radical members of the Minor Church to the sanctuary of Raków, where they could enjoy the protection of one of the most powerful magnates in the country.

The summer of 1569 saw a tremendous burst of activity on the pleasant uplands overlooking the meadows beside the river Czarna, one of the minor tributaries of the Vistula. Along streets laid out according to the modern plans of John Sienieński, scores of wooden houses were rapidly rising as more and more settlers arrived from all parts of Poland and Lithuania. They were idealists drawn from all ranks of society. A number of them were ministers of the Minor Church, many more than would be required to meet the needs even of a rapidly expanding congregation, but they did not expect to work as ministers in Raków. At that point they had abandoned the whole concept of a professional ministry on the grounds that it involved living by the fruits of other people's labor. Instead, they should earn their bread by the sweat of their brows and the work of their hands. Moreover, the church, they said, did not need professional leadership. Andrew Lubieniecki records in his chronicle of the period: "There were some who spoke against all forms of liturgy in religious services, pointing out that it was not right for any person to do or teach anything unless he had had a revelation from heaven." Kasper Wilkowski, writing as a hostile witness after his reconversion to the Catholic Church, taunted the Racovians with an account that is presumably not altogether without basis in fact. "You remember," he wrote,

> when you debased yourselves and gave up your ministries, expecting that the Lord God would inspire more worthy men, and you gave place to cobblers and tailors, highly praising their teaching and marveling at it and saying that you learned more in one hour of listening to them than during a whole lifetime with books. You can hardly deny this. But being unable to stand it, you had to turn to books again and order the cobblers and millers to keep silence. For you saw ... what a confusion they made, of which you are ashamed to this day.

By the Racovians' own account of themselves, they soon became disillusioned as they listened to sermons "by a gentleman from his farm, a peasant from his plow, a townsman from his last or shop or cask, exclaiming, 'I am bored; I don't like his talk; it does not edify me.'"

But this was learned only from experience. At the outset it was assumed that a professional ministry was not only unnecessary but immoral. The leadership in proclaiming such ideas came from three men who were themselves ministers: Matthew Albin, Jacob Kalinowski and Gregory Paweł. The last-named was the leading spirit of the whole Racovian enterprise in its early days, and its most eloquent spokesperson. He was a graduate of the University of Cracow and had also studied at Königsberg and Wittenberg. For some years he was minister of the large Calvinist congregation in Cracow, till following the debate at the synod of Secemin he rapidly moved into the emerging Unitarian camp, his views at this point being characteristically denounced by Calvin as "fetid." He soon adopted many of the Anabaptist positions, and proclaimed them with a strong personal charisma and greater emphasis upon emotion than logic, despite his impressive academic credentials. His enthusiasm was largely responsible for generating the wave of settlers to Raków, though he disclaimed personal leadership in the name of a full democracy for all, under the inspiration of the holy spirit.

The fact that Gregory Paweł came to the forefront of the movement at this point illustrates how strongly the current was flowing toward the Anabaptist emphasis upon feeling, intuition, guidance of the holy spirit, communistic practice, rather than the Humanist emphasis upon reason and logical analysis, and an attempt to reform the existing social order rather than abandoning it in favor of Utopian experiments. Paweł was, like most of the Anabaptists, a complete literalist in interpreting the Bible. To quote Zbigniew Ogonowski, it was his view that "the word of God ... had to be interpreted literally and believed blindly in every letter, even though the sense might not be clear or intelligible." In his own words, "Christian law does not consist of reason, but faith in the order and the teachings."

He did not, however, speak for the entire movement. In fact, he was vigorously opposed even at Raków by two other outstanding ministers who joined in the initial phase of the experiment but did not stay long, refusing to go along with the majority in laying down the professional ministry: George Schomann, soon to become Paweł's distinguished successor in Cracow, and Martin Czechowic, who left Raków to become minister of the even more important congregation in Lublin.

Besides the ministers, the 1569 move to Raków included a number of radicals from the ranks of the *szlachta*. By this point the teachings of the Anabaptists with regard to community of goods and refusal to accept public office had made sufficient headway to affect even some for whom heavy sacrifice was involved in putting it into practice. According to Lubieniecki,

> Many men resigned important civil offices, and the King gave them to someone else; others both gave up their estates and distributed the proceeds. And Ożarowski, a distinguished man, came to the King in council at the Diet of Lublin, publicly thanked him for his kindness, but said that he could no longer enjoy it with good conscience nor serve the King nor the Republic hereafter, and resigned to the King his right to Przybysławice in the district of Lublin, asking that the King accept it from him and give it to someone who could really serve him. The King for a long time would not take it from him; but he still insisted, saying: "You can take a thing from me by force, Sire,

> but you cannot give it to me by force." And thereupon John Firlej, Marshal of the Crown, at once asked for it, saying that it had come from his starosty of Kasimierz and asking that the King return it to this starosty; and so the King did.

This was only one example. Some of the *szlachta* freed their serfs, sold their estates and distributed the proceeds to the poor. It could well be that a belief in the impending end of the world (another widespread characteristic of Anabaptists) may have played a part in these decisions, but they were none the less a most remarkable demonstration of the sincerity of the beliefs of persons whose interests were very directly affected by the teachings to which they subscribed. One might apply to this situation the comment made by Karl Marx on the final gesture towards freedom and equality made by the *szlachta* in the Constitution of 1791: "The history of the world knows no other example of such generosity by the gentry."

One outstanding instance of such generosity was provided by John Niemojewski, owner of estates covering twenty villages, district judge and member of the *Sejm*. He resigned his office, gave away his property, and to the astonishment of his handsomely clothed colleagues appeared at the parliamentary session in Lublin in 1566 "in a mean gray garment, without sword, without wallet, without attendant, rebaptized just a few days before." Niemojewski was one of a number of *szlachta* in the first group of settlers to come to Raków, though he rapidly became disillusioned by the tone set by Gregory Paweł and left with Czechowic for Lublin the following year. He was a learned and eloquent man, one of the most outstanding among its lay leaders in the early years of the movement.

Naturally enough, the names that have been recorded from among the early settlers are chiefly those of ministers and *szlachta*. But there were many others as well. A contemporary record says that in Raków at this time "there were gathered many people from Great Poland and Little Poland who were of the same faith. These were nobility, townsfolk, ministers and other learned people, as well as a considerable number of foreigners ... Later many people of the same sect from Lithuania, Volhynia and other countries came to them."

There is little information about the foreigners, except that many of them were Italians. They took no prominent part in the debates and other public events in Raków during this period. The majority of the other inhabitants appear to have been workers from the towns, if one may judge from the handicrafts and industries that were rapidly established – ironwork, textiles, paper manufacture and others. Agriculture, of course, was important; there was also some mining and forestry. Unlike the founders of some later Utopian communities, they appear to have had all the skills needed to establish a firm economic base, as was in fact characteristic of the Anabaptist communities everywhere during this period.

Chapter 5

Fruitless Dialogue

In view of the earlier contacts with the communistic Anabaptists in Moravia, the Hutterites, the question naturally arises as to how far the Racovian experiment was a deliberate attempt to copy a Hutterite commune. No conclusive answer can be given. Documents are few, some of them are tendentious, being written by Calvinist or Catholic opponents, and the dating cannot always be determined accurately. However, it would appear that some sort of communication, however limited, between the Hutterites and the Unitarians was continuous. The Italian heretics who had taken refuge at Slavkov after the passing of the Edict of Parczów in 1564 sent back their reports. George Huntston Williams, in *The Radical Reformation*, is of the opinion that "possibly communitarian Hutterites were present as observers" at the Synod of Brzeziny in 1565. The next concrete instance of dialogue, however, comes at the Synod of Pełsznica, which convened in October 1568, less than a year before the founding of Raków. There was considerable excitement when Lucas Martinides Mundius, a councilor from the Lithuanian city of Wilno (Vilnius) who had relinquished his office and income in order to devote himself entirely to a search for the true religion, rose and gave an account of his recent visit to the Hutterite communities in Moravia. According to a record of the synod:

> There was also talk about the Moravian communists, from whom had come at this time a certain Mundius, a citizen of Wilno, enthusiastically recommending the sect of the communists, both for their government, and for the fact that they were said to be of one mind with our people *de Deo et Christo*, and for their devoutness –

> whom some believed with satisfaction, but others not much, and therefore there was a dispute among the brethren. Not until Mundius promised messengers from them to the brethren did they become quiet, waiting for the messengers, that they might learn all from them.

It appears to have taken a year for the emissaries from Moravia actually to come. The Hutterites were proceeding cautiously, as was their custom when dealing with alleged sympathizers. Their own records note: "There flared up and persisted in Poland a desire for truth, which however was as yet lacking in understanding and was fruitless." At that point, under the leadership of Peter Walpot, the Hutterites were at the zenith of their growth and influence. Their idea of dialogue was that others should learn from them how to do things; they were convinced that they themselves had achieved all that was called for from Christians, both in belief and in way of life. By contrast, the situation in Poland seemed confused, even anarchic. There was no unanimity within the Minor Church, either on theology or on practice. Another synod was held in March 1569 at Bełżyce, and although the records are lost, contemporary accounts make it clear that there was active and radical discussion of such matters as the duties of masters and servants, obedience to the civil power, distribution of wealth, business practices, hunting and pacifism. The fragment of the records states that in attendance were "many fiery brethren from the cities, towns and villages."

This ferment immediately preceded the colonization of Raków, and not until the autumn of the same year did a four-man delegation of Hutterites finally arrive in Cracow. After conversations with the brethren there they went on to visit Raków. They were, by their own account, very cordially received, and first impressions were evidently favorable; for four well-educated young students for the ministry were immediately sent to Moravia to examine the community and become familiar with it, as well as to learn a trade, in line with the current Racovian thinking that ministers should maintain themselves by manual labor.

Before the end of the year the students were followed by a much more imposing delegation, consisting of elders of the Minor Church, under the leadership of George Schomann, minister in Cracow, Simon Ronemberg, a highly-respected apothecary from the same city, and Jerome Filipowski, treasurer of the palatinate of Cracow and one of the chief negotiators for the Minor Church in dealings with other churches and with the king. These were all persons who carried great weight in the synods of their church, took the middle path in the debates about social radicalism, and were unlikely to be carried away by enthusiastic interpretations of what they experienced.

What they did in fact see produced a very mixed reaction. They were obviously disappointed by the theological orthodoxy of the Hutterites, which in itself would have precluded any merger between the two bodies, but they were also troubled by the authoritarian way in which the communes were run.

The records of the Hutterites confirm that the Polish Brethren were in fact initially thinking in terms of a unification of the two bodies. Their *Geschichtsbuch* records: "They ... brought a letter from their community to ours, in which they greatly praised our community for its system and organization, for which reason they wished to unite with us." That letter, of course, was written before the Poles had any first-hand acquaintance with the way of life of the Hutterites beyond the testimony of one or two enthusiasts. George Schomann, at any rate, seems to have been favorably impressed during the visit by the Hutterite lifestyle, if not their theology, for he recorded later: "We found a very good discipline of God's people, but all the sects fiercely defended the triune God." The impression the visitors made upon the Hutterites is recorded as follows in the *Geschichtsbuch:* "Their great worldly wit and wisdom, in consequence of which the Lord's work seemed to them crude and naive, could not be suited to the service of the poor and crucified Christ."

The impression carried back by the Cracow delegation must have been so discouraging that the brethren in Raków had extreme difficulty in accepting it. At any rate, they sent their own emissaries only four months later, together with a member of the radical congregation at Olkusz. Of them the *Geschichtsbuch* records: "They visited here for a time looking on things with a cold heart and then departed. They did not treat the matter seriously enough and so it bore no fruit." The Racovians when they left took with them the four young men who had been sent earlier, and who had spent the whole winter there. Their experience had not been very satisfactory either, for it was later complained that although they were good at learning and languages, they had been ordered to thresh wheat and chop wood.

The negotiations broke off with mutual disappointment, and soon the recriminations began in earnest. The way the Hutterites felt about the whole matter is well expressed in a letter written by their leader Peter Walpot to the Polish Brethren immediately after the departure of the delegation from Raków (May 25,1570). In it he expressed his indignation that the Poles had come not simply to learn from the Hutterites, but with the idea that they might also instruct them, by which presumably he refers to theological questions. "Your envoys," he wrote,

> did not come to consult us and to learn from us the correct form of the Lord's community, but rather to instruct us and try to bring us over to their side – a thing we cannot brook from those who have not yet abandoned their pagan, worldly life. They blamed us for being too much concerned about the possible lowering of our authority if we followed in your steps ... As we know neither Latin nor any other language, they considered us, in the depth of their hearts (which is a matter of indifference to us) too humble and contemptible ... Even if they did accept our authority, they need not imagine that our community would admit them because of their knowledge of many languages or their alleged learning which (in their opinion) is much higher than ours. They would first have to undergo trials and tests, just as we did at first, passing through tribulations, loss of freedom, prisons and hard labor.

Though the tone of the letter is so polemical, it seems reasonable to suppose that there was some basis for the complaints. Intellectual snobbery has not been conspicuous by its absence in latter-day Unitarian circles, and there is no reason for supposing that it was absent among the Poles either. Certainly they were persons of education and culture who could hardly have failed to react adversely to the low esteem in which the Hutterites held both. On the other side, moral snobbery was obviously a feature of the Hutterian mentality. They felt that they alone were living as true Christians, and that anyone who failed to follow the pattern they laid down was to that degree unchristian and hypocritical.

In a later letter to Simon Ronemberg, Walpot returned to this theme:

> While in one instance you praise us and declare that you desire to learn, ask for instruction and promise to give up all that hinders you on the way to salvation, immediately afterwards you boast of yourselves as God's children, whom God has also enlightened a little ... It is disagreeable to me to have you shower me with praises, and I value them no more than Christ prized praises from the Pharisees ... You call me the builder of Noah's Ark – then, if you are not hypocrites, tempters, egoists and disobedient unto truth – why do you not enter this Ark, outside of which there is no salvation? Dear Simon, look within and examine yourself ... You know, when you were with us ... the trouble was that you opposed the community and persisted in your opinion without any effort at correction, as you do even to this day. And as for the community at once governing itself in your way and learning from you, you are after all not yet confirmed in God and yourselves need to be instructed in the first principles of the words of God.

There was therefore a considerable degree of self-righteousness and feelings of superiority on both sides. The Unitarians regarded themselves as intellectually enlightened and as being able to discover for themselves a lifestyle that would be authentically Christian, while the Hutterites felt that they alone knew how to live as Christians, that the role of sincere outsiders was simply to learn from them, and that so far from theological doctrines needing re-examination, they did not even need to be discussed, having already been laid down once and for all time.

The last word on the Polish side at this stage of the controversy appeared in the summer of 1570. Its author was not named, though it has been supposed to be the work of Stanislas Budzyński, one of the more moderate leaders of the Minor Church who had little sympathy with the experimentation that was going on in Raków. He was evidently not a lover of succinct titles, for the pamphlet was headed "A TREATISE not against that apostolic Community formerly in Jerusalem and described and commended by the New Testament, which should exist among the true followers of Christ, but against such as has been recommended by one of the numerous sects which multiplied from the teaching of Jesus after his Ascension, known as the 'Communists' in Moravia. *Extra quam* – they say – *non est salus*."

Its argument gives a full account of what the Poles had found to criticize in the Hutterite communes. In the first place, the Hutterites had a completely authoritarian system in which the orders of the hierarchy of elders determined every action of each member. Freedom of choice did not exist. Secondly, they hoarded and accumulated vast sums of money. Everyone entering the commune had to surrender all personal belongings with no possibility of retrieving them if there were a change of heart leading to later withdrawal. Everyone had to work hard, producing more wealth, and rumor had it that a large part of this had even been loaned to the Emperor. Thirdly, members of the community were exploited in conditions of near-slavery. The elders lived and ate well, while the others had little to eat and toiled from morning to night, almost beyond the limits of endurance. They had less privacy in their living arrangements than the domestic animals. Fourthly, the leaders lacked true piety and sincerity. "Like the Grand Turk, they allow no one access to their separate apartments except those few of their members whom they have elevated to some lower grade in their hierarchy ... When our Brethren came visiting them for a few days to converse with them, a special escort was attached to each as though they were envoys from Tartary." Finally, when the Polish delegates wanted to have a theological discussion and asked for this to be at a general meeting of the whole community, the leaders compelled the people to work and refused to talk.

It may well be that many of these allegations had a basis in fact, though one might also wonder why the Hutterites should have clung so stubbornly to a way of life so dismally unattractive despite violent persecutions and forced migrations. It could be argued that as strangers in a foreign land they had no practicable alternative, and to a degree this was certainly so. The communes that had managed to survive on German soil eventually disintegrated. Even on foreign soil the same thing could happen if there were sympathetic neighbors whose religious outlook was close enough. After their later emigration to Russia, the Hutterites lived side by side with Mennonite communities, and half of them forsook their complete communitarianism for the more elastic and individualistic Mennonite form.

However, there seems no reason for doubting that within the Moravian communes the way of life expressed the consensus of the group as well as the dictates of the elders. The elders were doing what was expected of them by the system in the same way as the rank and file were. Totalitarian the organization certainly was, but it was a theocratic totalitarianism, and as such had a strong appeal to uprooted people looking for a genuine community dedicated to a Christian way of life.

Chapter 6

The Perpetual Synod

Why should the author of the *Treatise* have written as tendentiously as he did? It seems reasonable to assume that he had one eye on the Hutterites and the other on the Racovians, who at this period were, at least according to some testimony, attempting to build a communistic society of their own. Certainly they never had, nor could they have had, a close-knit authoritarian system like that of the Hutterites, but they were experimenting, or intended to experiment, with communal ownership of property. There is little concrete evidence on the subject. The Polish scholar J. Płokarz claimed that "there is no doubt that Christians in Raków introduced communal property (at least for a certain period of time), having set up a communistic community." But the sources upon which he based this conclusion were accounts by contemporary Calvinists, who may well have invented the allegations in order to discredit the Racovians in the eyes of the political establishment. Similar allegations, with no foundation in fact, were made with regard to Anabaptist congregations in Germany and Switzerland which never practiced community of goods nor even believed in this as a theory. The probable aim was to excite popular feeling against them by associating them in the public mind with the infamous communitarian Anabaptists of Münster, whose excesses had come very close to discrediting the entire movement.

Stanisław Tworek, in his detailed study of the early days in Raków, is skeptical about the allegations of communism. The intention may have been there, but the composition of the group made it impossible to put it into practice. In fact, he suggests that it may never have reached any more radical form than is to be found in church pot-luck suppers.

Whatever may have been the practice, it is indisputable that community of goods was one of the subjects under debate in Raków in the summer of 1570, when the *Treatise* first appeared. The Racovian delegates had just returned with their discouraging report on the Hutterite communes, and the *Treatise* was no doubt designed to reinforce this, for following upon its unflattering account of the Moravian communists, it contains an attack upon the whole idea of a community of goods. "In the lifetime of the Apostles" (runs the argument) "the disciples of Jesus who belonged to the community which believed in Christ owned property and possessions." There followed an ample quotation of texts to show that this was indeed so, with the conclusion that "the nature of the large-scale business of the communists in Moravia differs vastly from the early community in Jerusalem." The argument follows a line familiar in Anabaptist circles. Menno Simons, for instance, had maintained that although the early church in Jerusalem had for a short while practiced community of goods, this had already been abandoned as a failure in apostolic times. There was no need to try to re-establish a policy that the apostles had rejected. It was better to follow, as the New Testament advocated and illustrated, a policy of love and mutual aid.

The argument developed in the *Treatise* is that only by retaining private ownership of property and living in a normal but responsible and loving way in the world is it possible to show genuine charity towards those less fortunate than oneself. "Real love, by which the disciples of Jesus should be known, goes far beyond shutting oneself up in a room away from the world and giving one's possessions to another to be managed. How can we know that this other person will have as sensitive a conscience as God has given us?"

Though the main thread of the *Treatise* is an attack upon the Hutterites in particular and on economic communism in general, the whole concept underlying the establishment of Raków also comes in for adverse comment. Is it right to contract out, to leave the place where one has lived and worked, in search of a New Jerusalem? "Jesus, our Master, did not order us to renounce the world but to let our light so shine before men that they, seeing our deeds to be good and holy, should praise the Lord and be uplifted ... Surely this ought to show us whether it is better to live in retreat from the world, appearing to live a more peaceful and saintly life than others ... or to remain in this fallen world and behave as befits Jesus' steadfast warriors ... He is a poor warrior indeed who, fearing an encounter, retires from the arena and yet desires to be regarded as a valiant Christian."

The similarity of the very wording here to that used nearly a century later in Milton's *Areopagitica* is striking, but there is no reason for supposing that Milton was aware of his predecessor, for the *Treatise* was written in Polish and never translated into Latin. But the point it made remains: don't experiment with Utopia. Stay in society and work for its reform.

As a matter of fact, in spite of the early Racovian enthusiasm, it was inevitable that this was the policy that would eventually prevail among the Polish Unitarians. Neither merger with the Hutterites nor the creation of a community which would resemble a *Bruderhof* economically but not politically lay within the range of practicality, for reasons that are readily apparent. Apart from a willingness to take the demands of religion seriously, none of the factors that made for a successful organization of communes among the Hutterites existed among the Poles.

The Hutterites were almost all of them people from a very simple background: artisans and laborers, for the most part refugees from the Tirolean mining areas. They were now living in a country where they did not understand the language used by the local inhabitants and had few incentives to enlarge their contacts with people who were outside the circle of the faithful on board the Ark of salvation. They had no assurance of any kind of security outside their own communities. Religious persecution of a particularly vicious kind ruled out any hope of returning to their native land, and the population in Moravia was alien to them in every way. There were among them no educated persons with the humanist passion for individual inquiry resulting in new ideas. On the contrary, they had come from a background in which they were accustomed to hard work, submissiveness to authority, a low standard of living and a sense of social solidarity with those whose circumstances in life were similar to their own. The communes in which they were now living met their everyday needs and also gave them the feeling that as a chosen people living in accordance with the requirements of the Gospel, they were on the road to everlasting salvation.

The Polish Unitarians were different in almost every respect. They were drawn predominantly from the *szlachta*, accustomed to the exercise of liberty and leadership, well educated and imbued with a restless spirit of inquiry which frequently carried them to unconventional conclusions. This group set the tone for the whole movement. In addition to the ministers, who came for the most part from the urban bourgeoisie, there was a fair sprinkling of others from the cities. None of them felt personally oppressed by the existing social order. Their proposals for change were based solely upon what they considered to be the ethical demands of the Gospel. Unlike the Hutterites, they had no authoritative book to tell them exactly what those demands were, and in the exercise of individual judgment differences of opinion were inevitable. Their sense of political, social, economic, religious and intellectual freedom put almost insuperable obstacles in the way of organizing tightly-knit communes, and in fact their movement was destined to develop along quite different lines.

Those lines at first took the form simply of a shift of focus. If communism was not the issue, community was, and the question of what it involved and what limits were to be drawn around it continued to provoke constant discussion. The question of how entry into the community was to be recognized was one matter that was solved with almost complete unanimity not only at Raków but in the greater part of the Polish church (though not in Lithuania). And this was a decision on which there was agreement with the Hutterites. The rite of baptism was to be the form of initiation into the community. It was not to be administered to infants, who were in no position to make a personal commitment or even to understand what it meant. It was reserved for those who had reached adult years and had determined for themselves that they wished to become fully participating members of the community. By consensus of a great majority of the Racovians, adult baptism by total immersion became the generally accepted practice.

On other matters, however, there was no such consensus. During the first three years of Raków's existence there was a continuous state of upheaval, in what came to be known as the "perpetual synod." There was the question of whether the office of minister was superfluous, and some members proposed that every type of ritual or ceremony should be eliminated from religious services, in favor of the spontaneous contributions of the cobblers and tailors already mentioned. This too did not long survive, though it lasted longer than the attempt to establish communism, and was chiefly responsible for the departure from Raków of Czechowic and Niemojewski in the summer of 1570.

The debates continued. Stanisłas Lubieniecki recorded: "Neither by day nor by night was there any peace, but arguments continued with various participants, until some became converted, convinced by the points of view presented, while others held to their own opinions and later departed." For a while the radicals were fully in the ascendancy. Martin Krowicki, a more moderate minister who never participated in the Racovian experiment, commented wryly: "It seems to me that they envisage a God who discriminates among human beings, who rejects some people and banishes from his presence those in high offices, but who gives his favor to those people who are dressed in homespun, who wear ragged and dirty clothing or vermin-infested skins."

In the stormy Racovian meetings, tempers rose and there was even name-calling. Schomann recorded that "sad to say, people called each other Pharisees, Sadducees, Jews or atheists." Deplorable though this may have seemed to the gentle and cultured Schomann, in that age of invective it was pretty mild stuff. After all, Calvin had dismissed Castellio, who had ventured to disagree with him on the issue of toleration, as a blasphemer, a fool who mocked at God, an impudent wretch full of bestiality, and a dirty dog. As for Menno Simons, whom he had never met and knew only from hearsay, Calvin called him a conceited donkey and an impudent dog. Even less repeatable phrases were not infrequently used by Protestants and Catholics alike. Nonetheless, it was characteristic of the humanists to be revolted at such a manner of conducting a controversy, and that their own brethren in Raków should at times have descended so low was certainly one of the causes of disenchantment.

Concern about the way things were going in Raków steadily grew. In the letter quoted above, Krowicki continued, "exaggerated claims were made for Raków which came to nothing, and which constituted an affront to God, a laughing-stock to the people and a scandal to the Lord's church." Simon Ronemberg, looking back in similar vein, said that "there was more than enough confusion among the Racovians and amongst us all." Alarmed though they were at what they themselves knew to be happening in Raków, they were even more alarmed by the possible consequences of malicious rumors about what was going on there spread by their opponents with a view to discrediting the whole Unitarian movement. Enough things of an unconventional nature were actually occurring to give credibility to sensational rumors based more upon imagination than upon fact. Calvinists and Catholics alike assisted in the growth of such legends, some of which have persisted in the area right down to the present day. Even from Transylvania, Biandrata wrote to express his concern at what he was hearing.

It was evident that the attempt to organize a community of individualists on the basis of a full participatory democracy was breaking down. By 1572 the situation was approaching complete anarchy. Many of the disillusioned leaders had already left. It was obvious that if the situation were to be retrieved, someone would have to intervene with a strong hand and a clear mind. That is precisely what happened. Simon Ronemberg, the active and enterprising apothecary from Cracow, who had been among the earliest supporters of the Racovian experiment but had maintained his role as an elder of the congregation in Cracow, now stepped in firmly and reorganized the whole structure of the community along more conventional lines. A professional minister and a lay elder were appointed to manage its affairs, as was the practice elsewhere. To use a phrase coined by George Schomann, Ronemberg was hailed as a new Ezra, who rebuilt the ruined (New) Jerusalem.

But the new Ezra did not do it all single-handedly. Though he supplied the essential leadership, he could count on the help of prominent ministers and lay leaders in the larger churches of the movement, as well as the acceptance of a majority of the Racovians themselves. Scholarship now began to replace the inspiration of the moment as a guide to an acceptable lifestyle. Gregory Paweł, who has to bear a major share of responsibility for the chaos, continued to live in Raków and to publish controversial works. Together with a small band of disciples he waited for God's providence to usher in a new age. But in the meantime, life proceeded along more conventional channels. A variety of trades and industries provided the basis for a prosperous little town. Most of the ministers who had flocked to Raków now dispersed again, many of them taking positions as chaplains on the estates of sympathetic nobles in the eastern provinces who had held on to their property in spite of the recent denunciations of such action from Raków. The Lithuanian magnate John Kiszka took ten of them to his vast domains.

Chapter 7

A Time of Reconsideration

It was precisely at this time that one of the major issues that had been under debate for the previous three years in Raków's "perpetual synod" came to a head. This was the vexed question of pacifism. For anyone who is serious in searching for a genuine human community, the horrors of war must obviously stand as one of the most formidable obstacles in the way of its realization. Condemnation of war was unanimous among the Anabaptists, with the corollary that if you condemned it, you assumed a personal obligation not to participate in it under any provocation. In some circles the absoluteness of this prohibition was qualified to allow for extreme extenuating circumstances, but the Mennonites and Hutterites made no such concessions. Naturally, Gregory Paweł and his circle took the same stand, but Poland was not the easiest country in which to maintain it. There were times when incursions by Tartars or Cossacks could summon the whole country to arms to ward off the frightful atrocities perpetrated on those unfortunate enough to fall into the hands of such invaders. From the southeast the Turks were always a menace. The rising power of Muscovy posed an ever-increasing threat, as Sweden and Prussia did from the north and west. The terrible wars of the following century brought the whole country to the brink of disaster. So the question of pacifism was not remote and academic. It was fraught with far-reaching practical consequences.

The issue was first raised by Gonesius when he appeared in 1556 at the Synod of Secemin with his wooden sword, but the consternation caused by his theological views diverted attention for the moment from his radical social views. Although these were discussed between individuals in the ensuing years, they did not become a matter for public debate until after the formation of the Minor Church as a separate entity, in the period immediately preceding and following the foundation of Raków.

During this period it became the generally accepted view, at least among the Racovians, that renunciation of a worldly way of life involved both the resignation of public office and an absolute refusal to participate in war. Gregory Paweł took this stand as a matter of course, but so also did leaders like Czechowic and Niemojewski, who took issue with him on many other matters but agreed with him on this. So strongly did feeling run that those who were not prepared to endorse the pacifist position were not acceptable as full members of the church. No person holding public office could be admitted to communion at Raków, while according to Krowicki the Racovians condemned and consigned to hell anyone who carried a weapon.

The issue became one of immediate practical significance with the death of King Sigismund Augustus in July 1572. There was no obvious successor, for the country did not have the option it had exercised on such occasions in the recent past of electing someone from the same dynasty. The king was childless, and the most likely candidate to succeed him, his nephew John Sigismund Zapolya, Prince of Transylvania, had himself died a little more than a year previously at the early age of thirty. Speculation as to what might have happened had he not died so prematurely is one of the fascinating "ifs" of history. He could well have been elected King of Poland, for it was his successor in Transylvania, Stephen Batory, a man with far fewer connections with Poland, who was at length elected after an abortive and short-lived spell with a French prince. Since John Sigismund was himself a Unitarian, the story of the movement in Poland might have been quite different had he succeeded to the throne.

But as events turned out, Parliament took two steps during the interregnum which affected the prospects of the movement in different directions. Dreading a repetition in Poland of the bloodthirsty acts of religious persecution taking place elsewhere in Europe, and having so recently adopted a policy of mutual toleration in the Confederation of Warsaw, the *szlachta* agreed upon an oath to be administered at the coronation of all future kings, no matter what their personal religious persuasion might be. It included the following phrases: "I promise and solemnly swear by Almighty God that ... I will preserve and maintain peace and quiet among those that differ with regard to religion, and will not in any way ... suffer anyone to be influenced or oppressed by reason of his religion." In spite of opposition from the Catholic authorities, this did become the coronation oath. The question as to how far it might cover allegedly religious views that were political in their effect and could be regarded as subversive to the order and security of the state was never raised. In any case it became more and more of a dead letter as Catholic power steadily increased in the seventeenth century. But for the moment it promised security for the Unitarians.

It was otherwise with the second action taken by Parliament. With a number of possible candidates for the throne in the field, each backed by one of the powerful dynasties of Europe, the possibility of an armed intervention became a real one, so a general mobilization was proclaimed. Members of the *szlachta* were bound by long tradition to respond to such a summons to arms; in fact, the obligation to do so was the price of the privileges they enjoyed in the political life of the country, and severe penalties were prescribed for a failure to meet it. The Unitarian pacifists among the *szlachta* found themselves in an unenviable position. It could be argued that those who had resigned the privileges of their status thereby escaped the obligations, and as a matter of fact they were not subjected to any real harassment, though naturally they became the target of obloquy, including accusations of cowardice and treason.

Under these circumstances, it is not surprising that many of them embarked upon an urgent and searching reappraisal of the religious principles upon which their actions should be based. Some of them began to question whether they had not too easily espoused the interpretation of Christian behavior brought back by Gonesius from the now largely discredited Hutterites and reiterated by the radical communitarians in Raków. Had Christ in fact clearly condemned the bearing of arms and the acceptance of political office? Some of the Brethren did not think so, and to support their position they commissioned and published a book by one of the foremost among the humanist heretics currently in Poland during the course of his continuous movements around Europe. It appeared only a few weeks after Parliament ordered the mobilization.

The author was Jacob Palaeologus, a Greek, supposedly descended from the ruling dynasty of the Byzantine empire. He had nothing to lose by taking an unpopular stand politically, for his religious views had made him such a marked man that when he was captured by the Catholics in Moravia a decade later, they had no hesitation in sending him to Rome to be burned at the stake. But on this issue he did not feel the heretical point of view to be the correct one. Pacifism, in his opinion, was not only not a religious requirement; given the realities of life in this world, it was an irresponsible position to take.

The ensuing controversy became the central issue in the church for the next twenty years. In brief, Palaeologus argued that while aggressive warfare is morally indefensible, it is quite otherwise with a war that is purely defensive in character. In his words, "Christians are allowed to put on armor and defend the borders of their homeland for the safety of their own people and the annihilation of their enemies, whereas he who acts otherwise and refuses arms in such a case is both impious and unworthy of the name of Christian." The argument was a lucid and logical refutation of the absolutist position, but couched in such a bitingly sarcastic style that it polarized positions within the church. It was welcomed by most of the Lithuanians and by some members elsewhere, but the great majority condemned it wholeheartedly, denouncing it as a document written in blood and unworthy of serious discussion.

Gregory Paweł immediately issued a reply. This was not a piece of cold logic like Palaeologus's work, but an impassioned appeal to feeling and to the spirit of Christ. It broadened the issue under debate from that of participating in war to that of participating in political life generally, for Paweł saw the shedding of blood as an inevitable outcome of such participation. The only solution was to withdraw completely into a Christian community based upon different and higher principles than those of the state. Participation in public affairs should be limited to paying taxes and obeying all laws that do not constitute an outrage to conscience. Clearly, he was still looking for his model to the Hutterites, with their complete renunciation of all participation in the life of the world outside their own communities.

In the absence of such a closed community after the failure of the first experiment at Raków, such a policy would be difficult to implement. The church as a spiritual community could not provide a total environment for the life of its members in the way it could if it were an economic and social community as well. Raków now entered upon a period of comparative obscurity, as though the inhabitants felt that by lying low and doing nothing sensational they could live down the reputation the town had gained during its first three years. The most influential centers of the Minor Church were now in Cracow, already threatened by the growing power and pressure of the resurgent Catholics, and in Lublin, which until the turn of the century was predominant. But these were major cities, in which it was impossible for members of the church to ignore the social and political setting. The same was also true for the Unitarian *szlachta* scattered on their country estates. They too had to live on some kind of terms side by side with neighbors who had no sympathy with their views.

This being so, it seems likely that Racovian pacifism would have declined as rapidly as Racovian communism, apart from several factors which prolonged its life considerably. In the first place, the political instability and consequent threat to the country disappeared under the strong rule of King Stephen Batory. In the second place, the offensive language used by Palaeologus produced a backlash of resentment which prejudiced readers against his arguments. Thirdly, the reply that Palaeologus in turn wrote to Gregory Paweł's refutation of his original work fell into the hands of Paweł's supporters, who promptly suppressed it. Fourthly, the Lithuanian Unitarian Simon Budny, who at length got another copy from Palaeologus and published it, was unpopular both because of his support for the conservative Lithuanian landowners and because he was too advanced theologically for most of his contemporaries, arguing (as Palaeologus also did) that Jesus was simply a man and as such not entitled to any kind of worship. And finally, a new and powerful advocate for Racovian pacifism appeared in the person of Faustus Socinus, the most outstanding of all the Italian humanists, who arrived in Poland in 1579 and was almost immediately called upon to write a response to Budny's publication of the book by Palaeologus. Though he was not quite as uncompromising in his approach as Paweł had been, and though the presuppositions upon which he based his arguments were significantly different, Socinus at this point in his career was prepared to advocate and defend the Racovian view of participation in war and, to a large extent, the Racovian view of participation in public life.

But already, as Budny was quick to note in reply, the basis of argument was changing. Socinus, like Palaeologus, was a rationalist, and arguments advanced on this basis were subject to modification as the debate proceeded in a way that arguments based upon an intuitive certainty of the rightness of one's position were not. In the end, though Palaeologus and Budny were discredited, Socinus moved further and further in their direction. By the end of the century the uncompromisingly pacifist position had declined dramatically. The change is noted in the following passage from the so-called "unknown Arian chronicle":

> In the years 1595, 1596 and 1597, someone explained to the brethren, especially to the nobility, that they could with clear conscience possess the estates, rights and privileges of nobles, and bear arms, whereupon the aspect of the church completely changed, especially among the nobility. They quite ceased to be different in appearance from the rest of their contemporaries.

By this time Socinus had moved very close to the position advocated over forty years earlier by Frycz Modrzewski, whose book *De Republica Emendanda* was so highly esteemed by Budny that he published a Polish translation. Socinus was still a pacifist, but his pacifism was situational, not absolutist. Resistance to attack upon oneself he was now prepared to accept, though such resistance should not harm the enemy intentionally. Should the enemy be harmed or killed unintentionally, this is excusable. Participation in defensive war is permissible, but only with the understanding that there is no intention of killing.

To Gregory Paweł, who had died in 1591, this would have appeared to be a sophistical trifling with morals. To him non-resistance was an absolute demand without any regard for the circumstances, just as it was for the Hutterites. But Socinus was not a trifler. He too was aware of the sanctity of life and of the ease with which moral concessions could be exploited by those looking only for religious license to follow accepted social customs. But he was aware also of the infinite complexity of life situations, and of the need for religious principles to be applied with a sensitivity to all the dimensions of such complexity.

The differences in basic attitude between Polish Unitarianism in its first phase and in its second or Socinian phase take a variety of forms. Most fundamental of all, perhaps, is the change in the way the search for community is pursued. In the early period, with the influence of Paweł predominant in Raków and that of Czechowic (similar but not identical) predominant elsewhere, the ideal is that of a closed community separated out from society as a whole. The model was that of the Hutterite *Bruderhof* or, more explicitly, the early Christian community in Jerusalem of which the *Bruderhof* was supposed to be a later facsimile. The rigid authoritarianism of the Hutterites, together with narrow escape hatches at several points in their history when persecution seemed almost to have succeeded in wiping them out, enabled that movement to survive. But both the early Christians and the early Unitarians eventually found that it was not possible for them to shut themselves off from the world in this way; that, as Milton memorably put it, "to sequester out of the world into Atlantic and Utopian polities ... will not mend our condition; but to ordain wisely as in this world of evil, in the midst whereof God hath placed us unavoidably."

In the new Socinian phase the ideal increasingly became one of not contracting out of the world, but of striving to reform it in accordance with one's religious ideals. The turn of the century marked a turn in the fortunes of Raków. Having been almost forgotten for a quarter of a century, with most of its early inhabitants either dead or dispersed, with many of its early enthusiasms gone or so much changed that it would be difficult to see the continuity, with much of its early notoriety forgotten as the arena for religious polemics shifted, it was time for a new beginning.

Chapter 8

Raków Resurgent

A number of factors conspired to make the time ripe for change. The principal one was the change in proprietorship at Raków. John Sienieński, the original proprietor, had provided an open and tolerant charter and had indulged his wife's adherence to the Polish Brethren, but he had himself remained a member of the Calvinist body. His eldest son Jacob, in line to inherit his estates, including Raków, had married in 1598. His wife Anna, like his mother, was a Unitarian. It was probably no coincidence that during the following year Jacob moved over from Calvinism to Unitarianism, though he was a strong-minded man who would have worked through the issues to his own satisfaction before making such a change. He tested his new convictions as a participant in a debate between Unitarians and Calvinists in November 1599.

He had spent his childhood in Raków, but was still an infant during the tempestuous early years there. Well educated and eloquent in debate, he had already been elected to Parliament in 1587, and young as he was, had distinguished himself by arguing forcefully on behalf of the rights of the democratically elected Chamber of Deputies as against manipulation by the magnates. This stance was all the more significant in that he was himself the son of a magnate.

John Sienieński died early in 1600, and Jacob was now the proprietor of Raków. With all the zeal of a recent convert he determined to reconstitute the town in order to make it, if not the New Jerusalem of which the early Racovians had dreamed, then the chief center of

Unitarianism to serve the Polish-Lithuanian Commonwealth and beyond: a New Geneva or New Rome. He was prepared to invest much of the considerable fortune he had inherited in this enterprise, and began by replacing the modest meetinghouse that had been the Brethren's place of worship since the town was founded by a larger and more imposing one.

At the same time he was moving to establish Raków as the recognized center for the intellectual life of the movement, and with this in mind he invited a group of its leading thinkers to come for meetings to hammer out a consensus in updating their theological and social views for the new century. The first such meeting, for three weeks in the spring of 1601, brought a group of the most prominent ministers together with Faustus Socinus. Socinus was by now their acknowledged intellectual guide, although he was not prepared to accept the baptism by immersion that was required for full membership.

The next synod was invited to meet at Raków for twelve days in October 1601. This was much more than a normal gathering, for it included a series of lectures by Socinus outlining the cardinal principles of the revised Unitarianism that would become known as Socinianism. The synod also enthusiastically endorsed a proposal, supported by Sienieński, to set up an academy. The Bohemian Brethren as well as the Jesuits had already demonstrated how effective a good educational establishment could be, not only in providing training to potential leaders of the nation, but also in promoting their own interpretation of religion. The Raków academy came into being the following year, the necessary land and buildings being provided at Sienieński's expense. From the outset, it proved highly successful, drawing a distinguished faculty and students not only from all over the country, but from other parts of Europe. It eventually gained a widespread reputation as the "Sarmatian Athens." (Sarmatia was the mythical realm to which the Polish *szlachta* felt they belonged; only the name linked it to the real Sarmatians, nomadic tribes who had swept in from the east in Roman times before disappearing from history).

One distinctive feature of the academy was its avowedly interfaith character. Unlike the schools set up by other confessions, it was not only open to all, but expressly provided that students should attend services of their own faith and subsequently discuss the teaching that had been given them at those services. As a result, there was a wide diversity within the student body. Not only Protestants, but many Catholic families sent their sons there, and many of the Raków students proceeded from there to major universities in Germany and Holland.

From this point onward, nearly all the synods met at Raków, as well as regular meetings and discussions involving the leading ministers. Meanwhile, the position of the Polish Brethren in the big cities was becoming increasingly precarious. Their meetinghouse in Cracow had been destroyed by a mob in 1591. An attack upon Socinus three years later had forced him to leave the city forever; for the next ten years of his life he was the guest of his friend Abram Błonski in the remote village of Lusławice. By 1599 Alexis Rodecki, who operated the Unitarian publishing house, judged that it was time for him too to move out of this threatening environment, and the new and attractive prospects at Raków made this his preferred destination. The economic benefit this brought to the little town was enhanced by the addition of a paper mill to supply the press, which was productive enough to be able to supply markets in Cracow as well. Shortly after moving the printing house there, Rodecki handed over its management to his son-in-law Sebastian Sternacki, over whose name some two hundred titles appeared during the forty years of its operation. These Raków prints, most of them in Latin, were smuggled across borders in barrels and circulated widely all over Europe. They found a place in the libraries of progressive thinkers everywhere. Not all of them were Unitarian, or even religious; there were also educational works of a high standard, and books of poetry.

The new Raków was as open to the world as the earlier Raków had been closed. The nature of the town thus expressed in a striking way one of the great changes in attitude that had taken place within the Polish movement – the change from seeking salvation in a closed community to that of bringing salvation to the world at large. Accompanying it were other changes not so immediately obvious at a glance, but no less important for their long-term effects.

Gregory Paweł and his circle had been complete literalists so far as the text of the Bible was concerned. They drew from that text conclusions that were quite unacceptable in the eyes of orthodox Catholics and Protestants, but they were just as uncritical in treating the Bible as an oracle. The eighteenth-century critic Johann von Mosheim said of them:

> While in the matter of doctrine they take the greatest liberty with the expressions of Scripture, and pervert them in a violent manner to the defense of their peculiar tenets, they proceed quite otherwise when they come to prescribe rules of conduct from the precepts of the Gospel; then they understand the precepts literally, and apply them without the least distinction of time, persons and circumstances.

The second half of this criticism has a good deal more force than the first, for orthodox and heretic alike in that period thought they were drawing their "peculiar tenets" directly out of the plain teachings of Scripture. But the point is that the whole frame of mind in which the Scripture was approached was an oracular one. The Scripture was an oracle, and the task of the expounder was to work the oracle. It was not the only oracle. There were the oracles of nature too, which taught truths about human life and destiny by analogy. This was one of the favorite forms of argument during the medieval period and survived long after it. There was also the oracle to be found within oneself: the holy spirit speaking in one's own inward experience. Belief in this oracle was what inspired the abandonment of a professional ministry at Raków in the initial phase. In the same way, among the Hutterites the twin oracles of Scripture and inner guidance made it unnecessary for the minister to be more than a church administrator.

As the humanist influence made itself felt more strongly within the movement, this unquestioning acceptance of oracular deliverances faded. As far back as the second book of Palaeologus, although the author relied primarily upon the authority of the Bible, he poured scorn on the unquestioning literalism of Paweł. Palaeologus likened this to the folly of those who hewed out great crosses in the forests and walked the villages and towns wearily carrying them on their shoulders, so as to fulfill the commandment of Christ, "Take up thy cross and follow me."

But it is with Socinus that the change from an oracular to a rational approach became more noticeable. He too maintained an appeal to the authority of the Bible, but this was now combined with a direct appeal to reason. The teachings of the church, whether on theology or ethics, should be reasonable. The question of what should be done if the teachings of Scripture turned out to be unreasonable had not yet been fully faced. It was assumed that they were capable of an interpretation that would square them with the demands of reason, and this was responsible for some of the curious convolutions of thought noted by Mosheim. It remained for Socinus's grandson, Andrew Wiszowaty, foremost spokesperson for the last generation of Unitarians in Poland, to state clearly in his book *Religio rationalis* that if ever a clear conflict arose between reason and Scripture, reason had the last word. The Bible should thenceforward be regarded as a record of the ways in which basic religious principles expressed themselves in the words and lives of religiously-committed persons, rather than as a set of oracles.

H. J. McLachlan succinctly summarizes the Socinian theology as "a half-way house between medievalism and modernism." As such, it represented no more than a transitional stage moving towards the eighteenth-century Enlightenment, but it still marked a radical break with the past. Gregory Paweł, with his shuffling of oracles, had remained essentially medieval in spirit. Socinus launched a new approach. As Zbigniew Ogonowski puts it, "All dogmas contrary to common sense and reason were thought to be merely human inventions and harmful ... An inner conviction of the truth of some matter was still no proof of its truth, and the sole judge capable of deciding about the true sense of the articles of faith contained in the revelation was reason."

The final change to be noted in the evolution of thinking into the Socinian phase is the gradual abandonment of an absolutist view in ethics to a situational view, based upon a realistic appraisal of the actual facts in any given situation. Such a change runs parallel to the switch from an oracular to a rationalist approach in theology; it is in fact the necessary corollary of it. Relationships between person and person and between individual and community were to be based upon the application of the spirit of Christ and the demands of love, rather than upon a rigorous application of precedents drawn from a Biblical scene that might or might not be relevant to the current situation. Such a change was interpreted by some as a move towards moral laxity, and no doubt this was sometimes the outcome, as is always the case when the exercise of external authority is replaced by acceptance of responsibility for one's own actions. But it was the natural application of Socinus's belief in freedom of the will and of action, as against the predestinarian views accepted by the Protestant Reformers.

In none of these matters, whether the question was one of basic principles or of specific applications in ethical and political conduct, was there ever any sharp break between one period and the next. Nor was there unanimity at any given time. At each stage in the evolution of the movement in Poland there were those who maintained the attitudes and opinions of the early Racovians, and in the troubled years of the seventeenth century the uncomfortably persistent questions of communitarianism, office-holding, pacifism and loyalty kept coming back in new forms to vex the consciences of the Polish Brethren.

When Faustus Socinus died in 1604, Raków was moving towards the zenith of its vitality and influence. It was now without question the leading center of the Unitarian movement, the *Roma arianorum*. Of the forty-four synods held by the Polish Brethren between 1600 and 1638, thirty took place in Raków. However radical the theology discussed there, the community was no longer noted for its social radicalism. Rather, it became an administrative center where the archives of the movement were kept, an educational center whose academy was known throughout the country and beyond, and the location of one of the earliest public libraries. Its printing press published works exerting such influence that in Germany alone more than seven hundred refutations of Socinian teachings were published during the seventeenth and eighteenth centuries. The town attracted as residents many persons who valued this atmosphere; although Socinus was never among them, he was a frequent visitor and was actively considering a move to Raków at the time of his death.

Chapter 9

Unitarian Capital of Europe

For the first two decades of the seventeenth century, under Jacob Sieniеński's powerful protection, Raków's star was in the ascendant. For progressive thinkers it provided an almost idyllic setting, enhanced by the natural beauty of its surroundings. Jerome Moskorzowski, one of its leading figures, expressed his delight in lyrical lines:

> Raków, renowned for graceful springs,
> Circled with densely wooded groves,
> I give you songs composed in rhyme
> And praise your name in verse.

The profusion of activities promoted economic prosperity. As many as four hundred or more people from all parts of the country attended the synods, putting a tremendous strain upon the little town's accommodations but enriching the townsfolk in the process. Paper was produced for the press; various crafts flourished. Jacob Sieniеński, whose manor-house was just across the river from the town, appears to have poured a substantial part of his considerable wealth into Raków after he became a member of the Polish Brethren. Congregations across the country sent contributions to the support of the academy, which had no tuition fees and provided bursaries for the support of impoverished students.

The name of Raków became famous all over Europe with the publication in 1605 of the *Racovian Catechism,* in which the views of the people now coming to be frequently called Socinians were vigorously presented. Socinus himself had worked on some of the advance preparation of this document, though in its published form it was the work of three of his disciples. It presented a systematic outline of the views now generally held in the movement, with some continuity but with many major departures from those current in Raków thirty-five years earlier.

The Catechism repudiated the traditional Christian doctrine of original sin, which had been the presupposition of the whole scheme of salvation. If the first man Adam had committed one particular sin, as the Scripture described, this was not enough in itself to result in the total corruption of his own nature, much less that of all his descendants. It would be an indictment of the justice of God to suppose that it could result in punishments for the whole human race.

So baptism as a symbolic washing away of this supposed corruption was unwarranted. Here the Catechism echoed at least one aspect of the Anabaptist objection to infant baptism. Even for adults, this rite was only a symbolic affirmation of entry into a Christian community, a spiritual rebirth through bringing one's reason and will into acceptance of a way of life governed by the guidance of Christ. Such a way was the path to eternal life.

Jesus had a prophetic role in revealing to us the will of God and calling upon us to imitate him in doing the will of God. It was not through his death that he atoned for our sins; God freely forgives the sins of those who truly repent and endeavor to do his will. We have the freedom to choose to do this; the doctrine of predestination is rejected. Turning to the other roles of Christ, he has been given all power in heaven and earth, and intercedes with God on our behalf; he has therefore been raised beyond a purely human status, but is not himself God. We remember him in the celebration of the Lord's Supper, which is not in the traditional sense a sacrament, but rather a common meal in which we acknowledge our discipleship. Only the preaching and prayers which accompany the meal have any direct value to the worshiper.

The Church is not a specific institution, but exists wherever these truths are accepted and expounded. No institution can exercise authority over the individual Christian; only Scripture has such authority. Here again the Catechism recalls the original impulse that gave birth to the movement in 1565, when it was declared that in the true Church no one person could rule over another in matters of faith. There had been a complete move away from the teaching of Martin Czechowic, leader during the intermediate period, whom Simon Budny had called "the Pope of Lublin," and who advocated a much tighter form of organization. By the time of the publication of the Catechism, Czechowic had been deprived of his position and was living in obscure retirement.

Though famous in this way through its Catechism, Raków was still a small community, with a population variously estimated as between 1100 and 1500. This was a typical size for a Polish town in an age when the national capital in Cracow had fewer than 30,000 inhabitants and only a handful of other cities could boast even 10,000. The Unitarians dominated its life, though there was a small Calvinist congregation and a growing Jewish community which had its synagogue by 1614. The Catholics, who were also growing in numbers, were denied the same opportunity to build their own place of worship, which remained as a continuing grievance. But in other respects, the Unitarians were now relatively relaxed in their enjoyment of religious freedom, and the bitter internal disputes of an earlier time were no more than a memory. A variety of crafts and industries flourished. A hospital and a public bathhouse had been built. Most of the houses had their own garden; some also had orchards and farm buildings. A Scotsman named Thomas Segeth who visited in 1612 told a friend that on arrival there "he felt as though he had been transported into another world; for whereas elsewhere all was full of wars and tumult, there all was quiet, men were calm and modest in behavior, so that you might think them angels, though they were spirited in debate and expert in language." (The court records of the period indicate that not all the inhabitants could be mistaken for angels; there were assaults and thefts and drunkenness, though no doubt on a lesser scale than in other comparable towns, and the courts were inclined to impose lenient punishments.)

During this period a number of foreigners from many parts of Europe were drawn to Raków either by the academy or by the religious principles it embodied, and many of them in turn became leaders in the movement. A notable example was Valentin Schmalz, generally known as Smalcius. A German from Gotha, he was converted to Socinian views in discussions at the University of Strassburg with a Polish student. He moved to Poland in 1593 at the age of 21, married a Pole and became so thoroughly polonized that five years later, after a spell as a teacher, he was called to succeed Czechowic as a minister at the important church in Lublin. He participated in the seminars with Socinus in Raków, became minister of the church there in 1605 and remained in that office until his death in 1622. Together with Jerome Moskorzowski and John Völkel, he was one of the three authors of the *Racovian Catechism*. He wrote some fifty other works, and entered into a continuous series of debates with the famous Jesuit Peter Skarga, in which he maintained a rashly polemical tone. His home in Raków was the scene for frequent gatherings of ministers to discuss current theological and social issues, and he became a close friend of Jacob Sienieński.

Smalcius was only one of a number of Germans who became leaders in the developing Unitarian movement; in fact, the list of seventeenth-century Unitarian writers contains as many German as Polish names. Most of the rectors of the academy at Raków were German; so also were an appreciable number of the students. Since all lectures and even informal conversations were required to be in Latin, this international atmosphere was easy to maintain, and a wide variety of national backgrounds was represented both in the school and in the town.

Throughout this period the Unitarians continued to search for international and interdenominational connections that would lessen their vulnerable isolation. They had not completely given up hope of a rapprochement with the Calvinists, despite the rebuff they had received by being excluded from the agreement between the major Protestant bodies at the Union of Sandomierz back in 1570. But overtures in this direction were consistently rejected. Negotiations with the Mennonites in the Vistula delta were initiated in 1613, but only revealed too great a gap between the two bodies for closer relationships to be productively pursued. The Remonstrants in Holland seemed to be a more promising prospect, having actually taken an initiative in 1615 towards opening discussions. The Polish delegation sent in response to this was obliged, however, to turn back before reaching the Dutch border by an outbreak of war. During the next few years the Remonstrants were subjected to severe persecution. Some of them took temporary refuge in Poland, building a relationship that would prove very valuable to the Unitarians later in the century. But neither at this point nor in 1632, when a Polish delegation finally went to Holland for negotiations, were the Remonstrants willing to jeopardize their own tenuous degree of toleration by too close an association with the notorious Socinians, who were in any case considerably more radical in their theology.

Meanwhile Jacob Sienieński had become very active and influential, not only in the affairs of his own estates but in the wider life both of the nation and of the church. In a hotly-disputed and unruly *sejmik* (regional gathering to elect representatives) in 1600, where he was opposed by a representative of the greater magnates, he won election to the *Sejm* that was to meet in Lublin the following year. There he strongly defended the rights of religious minorities. In 1602 he published a little book denouncing the schemes through which the Catholics deprived other confessions of their places of worship, and attacking their attempts at censorship of literature. He demanded that everyone, no matter what their status in society, should be treated equally in the eyes of the law.

Such a stand eventually put him a very dangerous position. The king, Sigismund III, was a strong Catholic who went as far as he could to promote the interests of his church. By controlling appointments to the Senate, he was able to reduce the number of Protestants in it from forty-five at the beginning of his reign to no more than two at the end of it. There was widespread and growing anxiety among the *szlachta* over the ways in which his policies were threatening their traditional and treasured liberties. This culminated in 1606 in a *rokosz,* the armed uprising that was the legally recognized response to a king's violation of his coronation vows to uphold the rights of the people. Sienieński took a prominent part in the discussions that led to the *rokosz,* entering into detailed negotiations with Michael Zebrzydowski, Palatine of Cracow, who was appointed its leader. He tried to restrain the hotheads, arguing that disagreements with the king should be resolved through negotiations rather than by taking up arms. The dangers to the country from the outside were too threatening for it to dissipate its strength by internal conflict. When he saw that this argument was not going to prevail, he stood aside from the battle that followed, in which the *rokosz* was crushed by forces loyal to the king.

Events were to prove the wisdom of his decision. The country's resistance to external threats was indeed weakened. Moreover, there was some substance to Sienieński's suspicion that Zebrzydowski had personal ambitions beyond any role as protector of the people's rights, and was no more likely to defend minority religions than the king was. The difficult situation in which the Unitarians now found themselves was illustrated by the fact that although Zebrzydowski and his associates were pardoned and allowed to go unpunished, there was strong pressure within the royal army to destroy Raków, based on religious prejudice as well as on Sienieński's ambiguous participation in the discussions preceding the *rokosz.* For a time the threat was alarming enough for most of the town's inhabitants to flee to the nearby forests. But in the end the general amnesty was broad enough to spare them. The king was doing all he could to defuse the widespread suspicion that he harbored autocratic ambitions.

For his part, Sienieński wrote a flowery dedication to the king as the foreword to a new book by Smalcius expounding Unitarian beliefs. But for the next few years he withdrew from political activities, turning his attention to helping the Unitarians become better organized. He participated in many of the synods and made visits to congregations in all parts of Poland and Lithuania. He was a vocal advocate of religious toleration and of dialogue between the various religious bodies, though he could hold his own in debates with Catholics. In a notable debate in 1616, one of the Catholics facetiously referred to Jerome Moskorzowski as the "bishop of Raków," to which Sienieński promptly retorted, "He's not the Bishop of Raków – I am!" In Raków itself he upheld the rights of the various components of the population and authorized the elders of the church to mediate disputes between them.

The egalitarian ideals of the early Racovians were by now in total eclipse in their original home. Sienieński was the most powerful member of the dominant *szlachta* within the Polish Brethren. Not only was it in their economic interest to accept the status quo in the social framework; it also laid them less open to the charges of subversion, even treason to the state, that opponents had been all too eager to level at these heretical Unitarians. Their leading poet, Erasmus Otwinowski, celebrated the current stance in his poem *Obedience:*

> The Lord damned not the order of a wicked world,
> He wanted kings, lords, townsfolk, peasants.

At the same time, those who enjoyed a privileged position in society were reminded that it was incumbent upon them to act in a charitable and humane way towards those who did not.

But the earlier views had not disappeared throughout the country. In the congregations in and around the great seaport of Gdańsk, drawn largely from the bourgeoisie and working classes, they still survived, and found a forceful and articulate spokesperson in Christopher Ostorodt, a native of Germany who had come to Poland as a Unitarian convert in 1585. After two previous ministries, one of them in Raków itself, he had moved to the congregation at Buszków, just outside Gdańsk. He had always inclined towards the more stringent radical interpretation of Unitarianism, and was encouraged to move further from the current Racovian consensus by the environment in which he now found himself. This included not only like-minded Unitarians but also Anabaptists: Mennonites, and even for a while a group of Hutterites attempting unsuccessfully to set up a new commune. He endorsed the Anabaptist stance on war, the holding of public office and the building of a religious community governed by standards altogether different from those accepted in the wider society.

At the 1610 synod of the Polish Brethren in Lublin, concern was voiced about the threat to the entire movement by this resurgence of social radicalism, calculated as it was to revive the reputation gained during the first few years of Raków's existence, which had been exploited to the full by Catholic and Protestant opponents. Accordingly, in an ironic role reversal from the sixteenth-century Racovian actions, a high-level delegation was appointed to go to Gdańsk, led by Sienieński himself and including some of the leading theologians.

Ostorodt found himself in a difficult position. He felt bound to defer to Sienieński, not only because of his place in the movement but also because he had been a personal benefactor, having endowed him with a plot of land for a garden. At the same time, he remained unconvinced by the Racovian arguments. In the end, he uneasily agreed to submit, but only as an interim measure. His dilemma was resolved by his sudden death a few months later. Another delegation went to Gdańsk in 1612 to replace Ostorodt with someone more in accord with their views, and to silence if not eliminate his supporters.

Social radicalism was in fact to remain a recurrent issue for the rest of the Brethren's history. Thirty years later, again in Gdańsk, a prominent member, Dr. Daniel Zwicker, proposed that they adopt the full program of the Hutterites, including common ownership of property, and gained a strong supporter in Ludwig Wolzogen, a former Austrian baron. By this time the Polish Brethren were in such straits that their strategy was to ignore these proposals as far as possible rather than mounting a campaign against them. Zwicker and Wolzogen persisted in their views, but gained little support.

Chapter 10

The Axe Falls

As the century moved into its third decade, the religious, political and military environment for the Racovians began to deteriorate. Bands of irregular soldiers recruited for the many wars, often unpaid for months at a time, roved the countryside looking for loot with no fine distinction as to who was supposed to be friend or foe. On a number of occasions Raków narrowly escaped a devastating degree of pillage, usually at the cost of buying off the invaders with bribes. This procedure notwithstanding, some citizens suffered substantial losses. John Krell, rector of the school and subsequently minister in Raków, lost part of his valuable library. But the Racovians were not as unfortunate as the inhabitants of the neighboring town of Szydlów, who attempted to rely on their ramparts and fight off an attack. The whole town went up in flames, and its destitute survivors gratefully accepted large-scale aid from the Racovians whom they had been accustomed to regard as despicable heretics.

In 1621 the town was visited by another menace with an outbreak of plague, which carried off a number of the inhabitants. Against the human threats, at any rate, Sienieński was still able to give substantial though ever-diminishing protection, as the strength of the Counter-Reformation progressively increased, while the Protestants refused to make common cause with the Unitarians. He had returned to political life in the second decade of the century, managing to overcome the initial suspicion with which he was regarded both by the partisans of the king and by those of the ill-fated *rokosz.* He became a prominent member of successive parliaments and was even appointed on successive occasions to a Tribunal – the Court of Appeal for civil and criminal cases composed partly of persons nominated by the electorate and partly of nominees of the clergy. In accordance with his adherence to the principle of the separation of church and state, Sieniеński tried unsuccessfully to have the latter category removed, and his failure here foreshadowed the fate that would later befall those branded as heretics at the hands of the Tribunals.

As time went by, the threat to the radical vanguard of religious thinking increased. Throughout the country, the legal safeguards guaranteeing religious freedom were gradually being eroded, though technically they remained in place. Already before the turn of the century the "Arian" place of worship in Cracow, as well as that of the Calvinists, had been destroyed by mob violence. Socinus himself was assaulted and almost murdered by riotous students. Rescued in the nick of time by Catholics from the university's theological faculty, he was obliged to leave the city forever to find a place of refuge at a relatively safe distance, on the country estate of a Unitarian friend. The strongest urban base, that in Lublin, was likewise forced to close down by 1635.

Raków still seemed comparatively secure under the protection of its proprietor, but storm clouds were gathering around it. Although by the 1630s the population was almost half Catholic, Sienieński had consistently refused to make land available for the construction of a Catholic church. In 1633 the bishops refused to delay matters further, and proceeded to build a church to serve Raków in the nearby village of Drogowle. Sienieński found himself under pressure to pay tithes for the support of the Catholic priest in other villages owned by him. By this time he was in poor health, and he now had a powerful personal enemy in George Ossoliński, whose rising career had already made him Palatine of Sandomierz and Treasurer of the Crown Court, and on his way to becoming Crown Chancellor. Ossoliński was ambitious and ruthless, but unpopular among the *szlachta,* who suspected him of wanting to wield in Poland the same immense power as Cardinal Richelieu did in the French court of Louis XIII. Ossoliński hated

Sieniеński as a champion of the *szlachta,* and this was no doubt reinforced by a feud he was having with his half-brother, whose mother was Sienieński's sister. He was therefore glad to enter into an alliance with the promoters of the Counter-Reformation. The Racovian publications were banned in the country at large, and drivers leaving the town were searched to see if they had any of this contraband.

Under these circumstances, it was only a matter of time before some event would cause disaster to strike. Even so, its suddenness took everyone by surprise. In 1638 some teenagers from the academy were walking outside the town when they came upon a wayside crucifix erected by the priest for whom Sienieński had refused to collect tithes, George Rockicki. He owned an adjacent property, the boundary of which was under dispute between Sienieński and himself, and it was on this disputed land that the crucifix had been placed as an annoyance thinly disguised as an act of piety. The boys were unable to resist the temptation to throw stones at it and knock it down. The event was witnessed by some peasants. They reported it to their priest, who in turn informed Bishop Zadzik of Cracow, an implacable enemy of the Unitarians. Zadzik at once seized this opportunity, raised a public furor, and brought charges of sacrilege against all the Racovians before the session of Parliament then meeting in Warsaw. A commission of inquiry was set up to investigate the charges. According to established procedure, it should have reported to the full parliament. Instead, it reported only to the Senate, which by that time had an overwhelming preponderance of Catholic members.

There were protests against this irregular procedure from some Protestant members of parliament, and even from a few Catholics. Since Sienieński himself had been cited as an accomplice, many of the *szlachta* were concerned that their traditional rights were being threatened. But their scruples were overruled, and Sienieński was subjected to the indignity of having to swear on oath, under threat of execution, that he had not instigated the offense. No obstacle remained in the way of whatever verdict and sentence the Senate might choose, and it proceeded to pronounce judgment: the school was to be closed and never reopened; the Raków press and its prints were to be destroyed; and all the Unitarian inhabitants should leave Raków within four weeks. There could be no appeal.

Harsh sentences had not been unknown before in Poland, but they were seldom completely implemented on account of the division of powers between the central government and the very influential local *szlachta*, who in many cases ignored the rulings of the courts or parliament with impunity. In this case, however, escape was impossible. Times were changing, and the rights of heretics were becoming increasingly more difficult to defend. Many of the *szlachta* who had earlier embraced one form or other of Protestantism were now finding it to their advantage to revert to Catholicism, and the number of Protestants in the Parliament had declined dramatically. Sons of Protestants from the *szlachta* had been sent to Jesuit schools, which had achieved a reputation for their high standards of instruction and had incidentally fulfilled their intention of converting the non-Catholic pupils. Others converted under social pressures without this Jesuit exposure. The children of Jacob Sieniński, who were in line to inherit his properties, including Raków, had been among the converts; Sieniński himself was old and sick and died within a few months of the expulsion of the Unitarians. The estate passed into hands which would give them no further support.

So it came about that almost overnight, the chief center of the Unitarian movement in Europe was eradicated. Stanislas Lubieniecki, writing a few years later, described the sentence as "destroying the refuge of so many exiles, widows and orphans, and demolishing the seat of piety and of the Muses ... the very eye of Poland was then plucked out."

Some of the Unitarians moved as short a distance as they could while still complying with the decree, and built themselves a new meetinghouse on the estate of a well-wisher in the adjacent village of Radostów. (It lasted only twelve years, until this estate too passed into Catholic hands.) Others remained in Raków, ostensibly having converted to Catholicism but still Unitarians at heart. The perceptive Catholic authorities were well aware of this, and brought a monastic order to the town with a specific mandate to complete the work of conversion, a project that kept them occupied for the remainder of the century. The Unitarian meetinghouse in Raków was torn down, and on its site Bishop Zadzik constructed, largely at his own expense, an imposing Catholic church, which to this day bears above the main entrance a plaque commemorating the overthrow of the Arian blasphemy. On the ceiling of the bishop's palace in Kielce a large painting was commissioned celebrating the trial of the Unitarians and their banishment from Raków; it remains one of the notable reminders of the "Arian" past.

After the loss of the town, a number of the leading Racovian Unitarians moved to Kisielin, in a remote area of the Ukraine, where a pre-existing school was expanded in the hope that it could compensate for the destruction of the one in Raków. But the entire Polish movement was to survive only a few years longer. Persecution was now becoming fierce and sustained. Ten years after the Unitarians were driven from Raków, the country entered upon a terrible period in its history – a period generally called The Deluge. Disastrous wars swept across the face of the land, in the course of which the remaining Unitarians suffered badly, as did many others. The fact that the invading armies were composed of Protestants or Orthodox made it easier for Catholic apologists to equate Catholicism with patriotism, and they seized the opportunity to accuse the Unitarians of collaboration with the king's enemies.

Eventually King John Casimir, who had himself been a Jesuit before the Pope relieved him of his vows to enable him to ascend the throne, took a solemn oath that if he were to be triumphant in battle he would, out of gratitude to God, banish all the "Arians" from the country. Success finally came, and he carried out his vow. All the surviving members of the Polish Brethren were given the choice of conforming to the Catholic church or leaving the country by July 1660. The leaders scattered to various parts of Europe. It was from Holland, where a number of them took refuge, that their books were reissued and continued to play their part in laying the foundations for the eventual emergence of Unitarian movements in England and America.

An underground movement continued in Poland for many years, with exiled ministers taking great risks to re-enter the country and to serve the needs of their members. In East Prussia, where a number of the Brethren had taken refuge, they were given a limited degree of toleration on condition that they kept a very low profile and made no attempt to spread their ideas. Under these conditions, a congregation survived in the little village of Andreaswalde until early in the nineteenth century. Another substantial group made its way to join fellow-Unitarians in Transylvania, where one of the four Polish congregations they established lasted for more than a century before becoming fully assimilated into the Hungarian culture. Several descendants from these families made outstanding contributions to Transylvanian Unitarianism.

After the Unitarians left, Raków entered into a condition which gave it no greater claim to fame than scores of similar little towns throughout the country. Its population dipped as almost all the factors that had promoted its prosperity disappeared. Many of the houses stood empty for a while. More than a century later, a census in 1787 showed a total population of only 764, of whom 555 were Catholic and 209 Jewish. The Jewish proportion of the population was rising, giving concern to the Catholic authorities, and still remained substantial until the Holocaust during the Nazi occupation of Poland.

When the historian Earl Morse Wilbur visited Raków in 1924 he declared, "It is positively the wretchedest little town I have ever seen... The houses were unspeakably squalid, and animals running at large in the muddy streets and market place gave the town the appearance of a huge barnyard or even pigsty." At that time, it would seem, there was little local awareness of Raków's illustrious past, though a rich store of fanciful legendry was passed down from generation to generation. Some of these stories were collected by Tadeusz Bernat, local school teacher and amateur town historian. The "Herians," he said, were reputed to have been of enormous stature and strange habits. It was alleged that on one occasion, when there was to be a baptism (referred to by the Catholic inhabitants as a "dip") in the river Czarna, the dam gave way and the water vanished as the minister began the ceremony.

Some folklore had wider currency. For more than a century rumors circulated that the Swedish invasion of Poland in 1655, and that of the Transylvanian Prince George II Rakoczy two years later, were to avenge the destruction of "Arian" Raków. Catholic polemicists did their best to paint as dark a picture of the town in its Unitarian period as possible. As time went by, more favorable pictures began to emerge and there were romantic fantasies about Raków's past. In 1835 a German author, Wilhelm Brause, wrote a play called *Die Socinianer,* set in Raków at the time when the Unitarians were being brought to trial. There followed a string of novels presenting fanciful accounts of some phases in the town's story during the Unitarian years.

A more factual historical awareness accompanied the emphasis upon Polish history as a whole that was stimulated by the re-emergence of the nation in the twentieth century after a century and a half of being partitioned between the neighboring powers (Raków during this period had been in the Russian area and had been deprived of its incorporated status as a municipality). During the Communist era, attempts were made to raise the early communitarian experiment in Raków to the status of a pre-Marxian pedigree for Polish communism.

A revival of interest in the Racovian story was locally stimulated by Tadeusz Bernat, and at a wider level by a small circle of academics who had painstakingly pieced together the story of the sixteenth and seventeenth centuries in the town. It culminated in the celebration in 1969 of the four hundredth anniversary of the founding by the Unitarians. A symposium was held to mark the occasion – the first gathering at this intellectual level since the expulsion of the Unitarians in the seventeenth century. A monument in the form of a large boulder with an appropriate plaque was placed in the market square, now converted into a park.* The muddy streets that had so dismayed Wilbur were paved, and some of the old landmarks restored. Little now remained of what had been there in the days of Raków's greatness. Most of the old houses had been wooden and were destroyed in fires

* The inscription reads, "In the 25th year of the People's Republic of Poland and the 400th year since the establishment of Raków as the Arian capital by the Polish Brethren, 1569-1969."

and wars. During the Second World War the town was the scene of a desperate rearguard action by the retreating Germans against the advancing Red Army, and 90 percent of it was destroyed or seriously damaged.

Yet some traces of the past do remain. There is the so-called "Arian spring," an arched-over supply of pure water from the hillside only supplanted in recent years by water mains. Behind the church stands the original parsonage of the Polish Brethren's minister. The old Town Hall, dating from the earliest period, has now been converted into a public library. Place names commemorate the printing house and the students' quarters for the academy. Their longevity contrasts with that of many Polish place names, which have changed with political fashions; this appears to have happened with the name of Raków itself, which was rechristened Raków Ariański in honor of the four hundredth anniversary, but the usage has not persisted. However, awareness of past greatness is now general, and is used to give status to the little town in the present. The words of the seventeenth-century Racovian Wawrzyniec Bartnicki have come alive again: "If all else is lost, remember to preserve your renown."

Chapter 11

The Racovian Legacy

Despite the eclipse of Raków with the ending of its position as the "Unitarian capital of Europe," and despite the banishment from Poland a couple of decades later of the whole movement of which it was the center and symbol, its influence upon subsequent thinking and practice has been profound, though often unrecognized. It was in Raków that the tension between individuality and community was wrestled with in a form that challenged successive generations. It was there that the issue of participation or non-participation in a social order of which one could not morally approve was debated. It was there that questions of tolerance and inclusiveness both in religious institutions and in society at large found memorable expression. It was there that change and growth in theological, ethical and political thinking were promoted. These themes are lively ones to the present day, and deserve a more detailed exploration.

The breakdown of the negotiations between the sixteenth-century Racovians and the Hutterites was due in part to irreconcilable differences in theology, but it was also, as already noted, due to the incompatibility of the strong individualism of the Polish *szlachta* with the collectivist mentality of the Hutterites. Yet there remained a yearning among the Unitarians for a form of community that would not override their respect for the unique individuality for each person. Such a quest has manifested itself again and again in subsequent Unitarian history, sometimes purely in the realm of fantasy, as in Coleridge's dream of Pantisocracy during his Unitarian period, sometimes at a more practical level, as in the nineteenth-century New England experiment of Brook Farm. These repeated the failure of the earliest phase at Raków, and for much the same reasons.

Perhaps the best way to take stock of individualism as a perennial feature of the Unitarian tradition is to look at the person who articulated it most strongly in the generation following the expulsion of the Unitarians from Poland, John Locke. Locke's thinking had a profound influence upon the development of liberal thought generally and upon the development of the Unitarian movement in particular for the better part of two centuries; indeed, its effects may be traced till the present day. During his own lifetime, it is true, Locke took some pains to repudiate his debt to the Racovians, and claimed that he had not read their writings. His timidity on this subject is understandable in an age and place where persecution was still very real and he had at one point felt it discreet to go into exile in Holland after being deprived of his position at the University of Oxford. One of his enemies, purporting to describe the dying confession of the Earl of Shaftesbury, declared that "the earl ... talked all over Arianism and Socinianism, which notions he confessed he imbibed from Mr. Locke."

So Locke was on the defensive, and took cover in evasions. None the less, it is a fact that his personal library contained a very extensive collection of books by Racovians and Socinians, and he even placed a specific heading "Unitarian" in his library catalogue. To this can be added his close association with known Socinians and Unitarians both in Holland and in England, as well as the internal testimony of his own writings. His indebtedness to Unitarian predecessors as well as his influence upon Unitarian successors is very obvious.

The individualism of the Unitarian *szlachta* is carried one stage further in Locke. As his biographer R. I. Aaron notes, "His individual is artificial. He has no family ties. He tends to be conceived as a somewhat isolated being even when he enters into social relations with others. So also Locke's state is artificial. It is a community of free and independent individuals bound together by a compact into which they have entered freely for the better security of their lives, liberties and estates – and it is nothing more." That last sentence might stand as a description of the Polish state of Locke's day, though it would be hard to parallel anywhere else. The use here of the word "community" hardly seems justified. It is a society, not a community. The former is an arrangement entered into for limited and specified purposes; the latter is an organic whole constituted of members who find their fulfillment only through relationship.

The tradition thus filtered through Locke has lost important features of what the Racovian experiment had demonstrated, to the detriment of later Unitarian aspirations toward community. In seventeenth-century Raków the intimate communitarianism of the earliest period had been discarded as unworkable for persons who set such store upon personal authenticity, but it had been replaced by a powerful sense of solidarity that enabled the Racovians to support each other through the period of adversity into which they later entered, which often left them with little more than such personal support to share. Before they were reduced to this state, they had extended their help to others in need, whether in the neighboring town of Szydlów when it was burned down in the course of an attack by freebooting soldiers, or the more distant Remonstrants in Holland who were undergoing persecution by the Calvinists.

A rich community life developed through the relationships that were established, and the contributions freely made by individuals to the common life were remarkable. The historian Stanislas Kot described life in Raków during the first quarter of the seventeenth century as follows:

> The liberality of the Brethren for the work of the Church was extraordinary; funds collected for the common treasury covered the expense of the enormous productivity of the press, the support of teachers, of the school and of ministers in straitened circumstances, and also made possible numerous propaganda journeys to Silesia, Germany, France, Holland and England, where the emissaries from Raków by means of their publications and conversation won secret adherents. In return, adherents made pilgrimages from Western lands to Raków.

In the more rigid individualism promoted by Locke much of this was lost, and the outlook which developed among Unitarians often promoted alienation rather than community. The yearning for a closer and more productive sense of community never disappeared, but found little outward expression, with the result that those who valued deep and sustaining relationships might in the end sacrifice their aversion to dogma in order to find the fellowship they were seeking in religious circles which had a rich and sustaining sense of community, but adhered to traditional doctrines. Only in the most recent period have Unitarians moved towards redeeming this situation and recovering the full spirit of the Racovian legacy.

The perennial tension between the claims of individuality and those of community can bring positive or negative results. If each individual person cherishes freedom of belief as a paramount religious principle, then this can all too easily result in a downgrading of the religious community. Over the years, certainly in the English-speaking world within which the transplanted Unitarian tradition grew, the phenomenon of the lifelong Unitarian who seldom or never darkened the door of the church has been a familiar one. The small proportion of children born into Unitarian families who continued in the movement suggests that they were being taught, by example if not by precept, that true individualism and independence involved a downgrading of the religious community, the church.

If something of this kind happens, then there is much evidence to suggest that the outcome is not simply a collapse of community, but a collapse of individuality as well. An unqualified individualism has a tendency to lead ultimately into the very collectivist tyranny it seeks to combat. In disillusionment with the alienation resulting from stressing the encapsulated individual, people can throw themselves back into the arms of a totalitarian collectivism. This happened during the Reformation period to many who at first reveled in the sense of emancipation from the authority of the Catholic Church; in the end, they returned to that authority or set up an equally rigid one of their own. It certainly happened during the twentieth century, with the flight of individualists, disenchanted by their sense of alienation, into Fascism or Communism.

A cautionary comparison might be drawn between what has happened so frequently to Unitarian individualists and what happened in Poland after the expulsion of the Unitarians. The stubborn individualism of the *szlachta* gradually reached a level which paralyzed corporate action. Under the principle of *liberum veto* which became established, any one individual in the parliament could veto proposed legislation, and there were times when whole sessions were unable to enact anything. The social fabric of the country was weakened to an extent which eventually resulted in the disappearance of the state, partitioned between avaricious neighbors.

Community exists at various levels, but in general, the wider the circle, the more tenuous the sense of community. There has frequently been a desire among Unitarians for a church co-extensive with the nation as a whole. In Poland this took the form of endorsing the hope expressed by Frycz Modrzewski and John Łaski for a national church, though it would have taken a further step to make this broadly inclusive in theology. Thomas Jefferson is said to have expressed the hope that he might live to see the day when every young man in America would be a Unitarian. Early Unitarianism in Massachusetts derived from and profited from the fusion of church and state. In England this sentiment was even stronger. It was only with great reluctance that Theophilus Lindsey and his followers finally gave up the attempt to provide themselves with enough elbow-room to be able conscientiously to stay in the national church, while a century later James Martineau spent much of his time in his declining years working out schemes for a federal union of religious bodies that could become a non-creedal inclusive church and thus restore the unity lost through the schisms of the seventeenth and eighteenth centuries.

Contrasted to this was the concept of the "gathered church": a community of the faithful sharply marked off from society as a whole. This was the dominant view of the early Racovians, and the idea of a separation of church and state became part of the developing Socinian thinking. Here the difference between what can be expected of church members and of society at large, which in an inclusive national church is minimized almost to the vanishing point, is heavily stressed. Yet the question of how much involvement church members have in the wider life of society remains. For the Hutterites, a total withdrawal from the world into the enclosed life of the religious community was the answer. In the earliest period in Raków something of the same spirit prevailed. In defense of this, it could be argued that it was not socially irresponsible, that the force of example made a significant contribution to the wider world, as had been true to a considerable degree within the medieval monastic orders.

But in the seventeenth century the emphasis moved strongly in the opposite direction; it now lay not so much on salvation from the world as upon salvation for the world. The Brethren were urged to participate in society and to give it leadership toward positive goals. This set the tone for subsequent Unitarian social action, based upon the concept of the church as a morally-concerned community calling attention to social ills and shortcomings, but not seeking for itself the political power to impose its ideals. Here the emphasis upon the separation of church and state, as endorsed from the outset by the Polish Brethren, has continued. It was set forth fully and clearly during the Brethren's last period, following the fall of Raków, by Samuel Przypkowski. Przypkowski argued that the authority of the church was spiritual; that of the state coercive.

> In the same Christian society there may and actually do exist parallel systems, different and apparently contradictory. One is founded on equality of persons and the absence of coercive authority; the other on difference between persons and the existence of compulsion. The one system is that of the Church, the other that of the State. Both when the State with compulsory authority encroaches on the government of the Church, and when the Church takes the sword which God himself has entrusted to the civil authority out of its hands, there is a violation of justice.

But at the time of his writing the tide was moving strongly in the opposite direction. The Counter-Reformation was triumphing in Poland with its principle that there should be a single authority, that of the One True Church, and that the State should use its resources to implement that Church's requirements. Though the views expressed by these early Unitarians were eventually to become the foundation for later multicultural democratic constitutions, medieval totalitarianism still exercised too strong a sway in the seventeenth century for their organized movement to survive.

Another aspect of the same issues comes to the fore when the question under discussion is that of the degree of toleration to be expected from either state or church. Looking back in the perspective of more than two centuries, Lord Acton (himself a Catholic) wrote: "The true apostles of toleration are not those who sought protection for their own beliefs, or who had none to protect; but men to whom, irrespective of their cause, it was a political, a moral, a theological dogma, a question of conscience involving both religion and policy. Such a man was Socinus." The outstanding contribution here made not only by Socinus himself but by the Polish Brethren in general was widely recognized by those who saw it in a much less favorable light than did Lord Acton. For example, Pierre Jurieu, himself a victim of fierce intolerance which led to his exile as leader of the Huguenot exiles in Holland, referred to universal toleration as "that Socinian dogma, the most dangerous of the dogmas of the Socinian sect."

The rise of the Polish Brethren took place in the most tolerant country in Europe during Poland's Golden Age. The declaration of the Confederation of Warsaw in 1573 placed all forms of religion on the same footing, referring to them all as *dissidentes* and guaranteeing peace between them. But within half a century the term *dissidentes* had become restricted to non-Catholics – the Catholic church was regarded as the established religion, and even those arguing forcefully for toleration of dissenters, as the prominent Racovian John Krell did in 1632, conceded a special status to Catholics as holding the reins of power. Before the end of the century, much of Polish tolerance had disappeared. The country had moved closer to the conditions elsewhere in Europe, though repression was not as extreme as in some places.

It was in lands further west that the seeds sown by the Socinians eventually found more fertile soil. John Krell's grandson, Samuel, was a friend of John Locke, whose *Letters on Toleration* were to be a significant and influential contribution to the rise of more tolerant forms of society. His contemporary John Milton, also influenced by Racovian literature, likewise wrote memorably in support of the same principle. Tolerance, claimed Earl Morse Wilbur when he came to assess the data for his massive *History of Unitarianism* early in the twentieth century, was one of the movement's three perennial leading principles, along with "complete mental freedom in religion" and "the unrestricted use of reason in religion"; moreover, "the first and most essential of its three controlling principles ... is that of generous tolerance of differing views."

Part of the concept of toleration, as its enemies clearly saw, was the principle that no one can be so sure of the completeness and finality of their own understanding of truth as to dismiss or suppress those with a different understanding. The fierceness with which Catholics and Protestants alike clung to the positions they had staked out in the sixteenth century was an index of their desperate search for security in an age of turbulent change. This may be contrasted with the acceptance of change and growth as a normal and desirable process that is expressed in the *Testament* of George Schomann, minister for some years of the Polish Brethren's congregation in Cracow. Addressing himself to his sons and grandsons, he wrote: "I have reached the true catholic faith by way of Catholicism, Lutheranism, Calvinism and Anabaptism. If in the future an even more pure church were to emerge, join it!"

The same spirit was expressed strikingly in the following century through the revisions of the *Racovian Catechism,* by contrast with the unchanging articles of faith of the Lutherans and Calvinists. In their preface to the edition of 1665, published in Amsterdam after the expulsion from Poland, the editors wrote: "While we compose a catechism, we prescribe nothing to anyone; while we express our own view, we oppress no one. Let each be free to express his own mind in religion ... We do not think that we need blush if our Church advances in some things. We ought not in every case to cry out, 'We believe, I stand fast in the ranks, here I plant my foot, I will not allow myself to be moved from here.'"

There could, however, be differences of opinion as to whether in this case the change was really an advance. In terms of the evolution of Unitarian thinking in general, the theological changes in the revised catechism represented a retreat from the original edition – an outcome of the influence of the Dutch Remonstrants, who while radical by overall Protestant standards, were more traditional in their theology than the Polish Brethren had been in their heyday. But the acceptance of the evolution of ideas as a natural process, no less than the specific beliefs arrived at in the course of this process, caused the Socinians to be looked upon as a dangerous menace by the custodians of closed systems of religion in the seventeenth and eighteenth centuries. In their taking such a stance, these early Unitarians were beginning a process that not only continued productively in their own tradition, but gradually came to be more widely (though not universally) accepted.

Both in their theology and in their social and political attitudes, the emerging Unitarians had to concern themselves with the context within which they were working. How far could one push the limits of what those around them would be prepared to tolerate without provoking a destructive backlash? It was this very issue that Faustus Socinus debated at length with the Transylvanian Unitarian leader Francis Dávid. For Dávid it was of paramount importance to state openly and unequivocally what one had come to believe to be true. Having reached the conclusion that Jesus was a man and not a god, it seemed self-evident that Jesus should not be invoked in prayer, and he said so. Socinus was unable to persuade him otherwise, and the result was that Dávid ended his days in a dungeon. Palaeologus and Simon Budny articulated the same views; the former was burned at the stake by the Catholics and the latter was excommunicated by the leaders of the Polish Brethren and spent the rest of his life in obscurity. It did not pay to move too far ahead of the society within which one was placed.

It might be unfair to Socinus to claim that this was his conscious motivation in maintaining the precarious position that although Jesus was not God, he had been exalted to a position which made it appropriate to address him in prayer – that this, indeed, was what marked a Christian off from a Jew. But certainly the social context put a brake upon Unitarian thinking in general. If one could express oneself in terms that sounded not too far removed from the accepted standards of orthodoxy, one might hope to have better chances of survival – though the custodians of the established doctrines often saw minor deviations in much the same light as major ones.

The same might be said for the retreat from the earlier Racovian pacifism. This time it was Budny who championed the views of the established order against the unpopular but principled stand taken by Gregory Paweł and Martin Czechowic. Socinus initially sided with the pacifists, but ultimately modified his position, though he never went so far as Budny in supporting active participation in defensive warfare. At the end of his life he was still wrestling with the dilemmas in which he found himself. According to the record of the Colloquium he conducted at Raków in 1601, he was teaching that it is not permitted for Christians to be involved in war. However, under the existing circumstances in the country, an outright refusal to answer a call to arms would open a man to charges of being a traitor, and subject him to penalties that would reduce his family to shameful poverty. Therefore, he may answer the call to arms, but "when it comes to battle, the Christian can be there but may not kill anyone nor think of killing anyone." Someone raised the objection that this "would be simulation, if I should do all those things and nevertheless not have in mind to kill anybody." Socinus responded, "Not all simulation is a sin," adding that his advice is given with the present conditions in the country in mind. If they were different, "other counsels would be contrived." It is easy to charge him with convoluted logic, but not so easy to arrive at an alternative that does justice to all the moral issues involved.

As with so many of the questions debated by these early Unitarians, whether in speculative theology, political theory, or practical conduct, we may be no nearer a totally satisfactory consensus today than they were four centuries ago. These are subjects that still demand examination, and at least some attempt to arrive at conclusions that seem valid for us under the conditions of today. In such an attempt we may find guidance and support from the Racovian demand for authenticity in thinking, a firm grasp of our values, and courageous action.

Acknowledgments and Notes

My own first-hand acquaintance with Raków, now extending to four visits, began when my wife and I visited the little town in 1969. Three years later we returned to become, so far as we are aware, the first Unitarians to spend a night under a Raków roof since the seventeenth century. I am much indebted to our gracious host at that time, the late Tadeusz Bernat, for information and materials.

My chief indebtedness, however, is to literary sources. This book makes no pretence to being a piece of original scholarship based upon research into original documents. I gratefully acknowledge the work of those who have done such research. My excuse for reworking the fruits of their labors is that these are for the most part available only in academic publications not readily accessible, and often in languages which would serve as a barrier to most English-speaking readers. I have not burdened my own text with the voluminous footnotes customary in academic work. These are usually of interest only to those who wish to pursue a subject in much greater depth, and readers in this category are referred to the following listing of my major sources. The interpretations placed upon events, however, are my own.

The principal books consulted are:

Domenico Caccamo, *Eretici Italiani in Moravia, Polonia, Transilvania* (Florence, 1970)

Stanisław Cynarski (ed.), *Raków Ognisko Arianizmu* (Cracow, 1968)

Norman Davies, *God's Playground: A History of Poland* (Oxford, 1981)

Ambroise Jobert, *De Luther à Mohila* (Paris, 1974)

Peter James Klassen, *The Economics of Anabaptism* (The Hague, 1964)

Stanislas Kot, *Socinianism in Poland* (Boston, 1957)

Stanislas Lubieniecki, *History of the Polish Reformation*, translated and interpreted by George Huntston Williams (Minneapolis, 1995)

Daniel Stone, *The Polish-Lithuanian State,* 1386-1795 (Seattle, 2001)

Lech Szczucki (ed.), *Wokoł Dziejów i Tradycji Arianizmu* (Warsaw, 1971)

Janusz Tazbir, *Reformacja, Kontrreformacja, Tolerancja* (Wrocław, 1996)

Piotr S. Wandycz, *The Price of Freedom* (London, 1992)

Earl Morse Wilbur, *A History of Unitarianism,* vol. 1 (Cambridge, MA, 1945)

George Huntston Williams, *The Radical Reformation* (Philadelphia, 1962)

———. *The Polish Brethren* (Cambridge, MA, 1980)

A word needs to be added about the names of persons and places, which in the original Polish can at times be daunting to the English-speaking reader. Some names have familiar English or Latin equivalents, and these I have generally used, but such equivalents are not always available, and there is no substitute for the original. For instance, Cracow and Warsaw are familiar anglicizations, but none are available for the smaller places. It is easy to render the name of Grzegorz Paweł as Gregory Paweł (or Gregory Paul), or of Fausto Sozzini (Faust Socyn) as Faustus Socinus, but no such option is available for Samuel Przypkowski or Jan Niemojewski. It needs to be borne in mind that others writing in English may have adopted different criteria, so that names appearing in one form here may appear in other forms elsewhere (a number of forms in Polish, according to the grammatical case). I have followed the practice of some other writers in using an English equivalent, where available, for the first name of persons, but keeping the surname in its Polish form.

In working from Polish texts, I gladly acknowledge the help given by persons whose grasp of the language is much more fluent than my own: Julian Leszczyński, Irma Zaleska, and Ann Weetman. They have saved me hours of work and resolved riddles beyond my understanding. Finally, I am grateful to Professor Daniel Stone of the University of Winnipeg for reading the entire text and for helpful suggestions.

Phillip Hewett

About the Author

Phillip Hewett is minister emeritus of the Unitarian Church of Vancouver. Born and raised in Dorchester, England, he served in the R.A.F. during World War II. He studied at Exeter College and Manchester College, Oxford University (B.A., 1949, M.A., 1951) and the Harvard Divinity School (S.T.M., 1953). He received the S.T.D. from the Starr King School for Ministry in 1969. In 1951 he married Margaret Smith of London, England. He served churches in Montreal, Quebec (1953-54); Ipswich, England (1954-56); Vancouver, British Columbia (1956-91); and Victoria, British Columbia (1991-92). He has also served for short terms congregations in St. Catharines, Ontario; Adelaide, South Australia; and Auckland, New Zealand.

Hewett has written a number of books introducing Unitarianism, including *An Unfettered Faith: the Religion of a Unitarian* (1956), *On Being a Unitarian* (1968), and *The Unitarian Way* (1985). His principal historical work is *Unitarians in Canada* (1978, 2nd edition 1995). He is a contributor to the *Canadian Encyclopedia,* the *Dictionary of Canadian Biography,* and the *Dictionary of Unitarian Universalist Biography.* He has been president of both the British and Canadian Unitarian Historical Societies and vice president of the Unitarian Universalist Historical Society. He has also served three terms on the board of the Canadian Unitarian Council.

Hewett is a strong advocate for the environment, family planning, disarmament, and peace. Since 1952 he has been active in the International Association for Religious Freedom (IARF). In 1983 the American chapter of IARF presented Phillip and Margaret Hewett a joint award for Outstanding Service to International Liberal Religion. In 1992 he was given the Unitarian Universalist Association annual award for distinguished service.